apocalypse (ə pok'ə lips) n. 1. See Revelation of St. John the Divine. 2. any of a class of Jewish or Christian writings that appeared from about 200 B.C. to A.D. 350 and were assumed to make revelations of the ultimate divine purpose. 3. revelation; discovery; disclosure.

apocalyptic (ə pok'ə lip'tik) adj. 1. of or like an apocalypse; affording a revelation of prophecy. 2. pertaining to the Apocalypse or biblical book of Revelation. 3. presaging imminent disaster and total or universal destruction: *the apocalyptic vision of some contemporary writers.*

apocalypticism (ə pok'ə lip'ti siz'əm) n. Theol. 1. any doctrine concerning the end of the temporal world, esp. one that is based on the supposed prophetic passages in the Revelation of St. John the Divine. 2. the millennial doctrine of the Second Advent and personal reign of Jesus Christ on earth.

—from *The Random House Dictionary of the English Language*

THE END!

A Portable
APOCALYPSE

A Quotable Companion to the
End of the World

Compiled and Edited by

ALLAN APPEL

RIVERHEAD BOOKS, NEW YORK

Riverhead Books
Published by The Berkley Publishing Group
A member of Penguin Putnam Inc.
375 Hudson Street
New York, New York 10014

First edition: January 1999

The Penguin Putnam Inc. World Wide Web site address is
http://www.penguinputnam.com

Library of Congress Cataloging-in-Publication Data

A portable apocalypse / compiled and edited by Allan Appel. —1st
   Riverhead trade paperback ed.
      p.   cm.
   ISBN 1-57322-714-5
      1. End of the world—Quotations, maxims, etc.   2. Quotations,
English.   I. Appel, Allan.
PN6084.E53P67   1999
001.9—dc21
                                                          98-41789
                                                          CIP

Printed in the United States of America

10 9 8 7 6 5 4 3 2 1

It makes little difference—though it makes some—whether you believe the age of the world to be six thousand years or five thousand million years, whether you think time will have a stop or that the world is eternal; there is still a need to speak humanly of a life's importance in relation to it—a need in the moment of existence to belong, to be related to a beginning and to an end.

—Frank Kermode,
from *The Sense of an Ending: Studies in the Theory of Fiction*

ACKNOWLEDGMENTS

It is surprising how many doomsayers, jeremiahs, or just regular people with a truly gallows sense of humor or just plain serious concern about the fate of our world I found during the course of doing this book. I will call these friends by a word that does not yet exist in the dictionary: apocalyptists; this neologism or something like it is sure to enter the language by the year 2000. I want to thank them for their help and encouragement—the latter equally as vital as the former in a project that immersed me daily and over a long period of time in ideas and images that one encounters more often than not in major nightmares between three and four in the morning. Please understand, even if I didn't use everything you suggested, don't worry, it's not the end of the world.

First, thank you to my daughter, Sophia, who helped name this book. To my son, Nathaniel, who leaned heavily on me as I edited, and my nephew, James Appel, who assisted in the computer-based research. And many thanks to my various personal apocalyptists: William Beavers; Allen Bergson; Jean

Boorsch; my wife, Suzanne Boorsch; Peggy Brown; Nita Colgate; Joan Corcoran; Gloria Friedman; Eileen Gillooly; Charles Hays; my agent, Lew Grimes; Marc Kaminsky; Stuart Kramer; Peter Minichiello; Chris Platt; Belinda Plutz; Dan Polin; and Nancy Larson Shapiro. Thanks also to my many friends at the Museum of Jewish Heritage.

Finally, because the end of the world is a subject vast in scope, tradition, and complexity, I consulted many works of scholarship. I am particularly indebted to the following: *Visions of the End: Apocalyptic Traditions in the Middle Ages* and *Antichrist: Two Thousand Years of the Human Fascination with Evil*, both by Bernard McGinn, arguably the major contemporary scholar in the field; *When Time Shall Be No More* by Paul Boyer; and *Century's End: A Cultural History of the Fin de Siècle* by Hillel Schwartz. Also many thanks for the dark inspiration of two novels and a meditation—Don DeLillo's *White Noise*, Walker Percy's *The Second Coming*, and Jonathan Schell's *The Fate of the Earth*—my trusty companions throughout this project. The amateur—or serious—apocalyptist is encouraged to consult these books and the many others in the field. But hurry. One never knows.

INTRODUCTION

As this book was going to press I received a remarkable message. It came via the Internet, with no address of origin. After I printed it, my computer froze. The lights flickered. It was eerie. Perhaps even, dare I say it, apocalyptic.

I had been intending to write a long erudite introduction to this book—to explain that "apocalypse" began as a Greek word meaning "revelation of that not previously known," how it then spent centuries primarily attached to the alleged secrets of the Book of Revelation, and how it evolved into a term applied to yesterday's hurricane, tomorrow's nuclear disaster, and today's E-mail. I was going to discuss the perhaps surprising fact that the idea of the apocalypse is central to Christianity, more peripheral in Judaism and Islam, and nearly absent in Asian religions and philosophies.

But then the E-mail came, and I was dumbstruck. I decided that the A to Z of apocalyptic quips and quotes, songs and sayings, poems and portents that you hold in your hands speaks for itself. From "A" for Antichrist to "D" for Devil, to "M" for Millerites and "R" for Rapture, here is a self-evident crash course in the central apocalyptic themes. And as for the rest—"N" for New Jersey, "G" for Germs, "M" for Mail Order, and "V" for Virtual Reality—they are pure fun! The E-mail was suddenly clear: Words are, at best, shaky servants of our meanings. And they are perhaps particularly prone to fail us in matters apocalyptic.

This is what it said:

To: Allan Appel
From: Isaiah, John of Patmos, Isaac Newton, Emily Dickinson, and Jim Morrison, on behalf of all you have aroused and disturbed by quoting us in your forthcoming compendium, A *Portable Apocalypse*
Message: KABOOM UGH MY GOD GRRRRRAAAAH-GLORYWOWPOW MY LORD MY LORD POW CRAAACK!!!! YIPES 'TIL WE MEET AGAIN THE LIGHT THE LIGHT GLORY! GOTCHA!

A hoax or a ploy? A dream? You never know. For even if this book were as thick as the Bible, the Upanishads, and the unabridged works of Nostradamus stitched together, it still couldn't do justice to all the ink spilled in the noble, poetic, profound, funny and—let's face it—sometimes lunatic obsession with coming to terms with our ultimate demise.

So for now, until the locusts and brimstone start falling from the sky, you can slip this guide into your pocket, banter with the best of them at cocktail parties, and check the weather advisories for high winds and rough seas. And if things start looking particularly grim, simply recall Hotspur's cri de coeur from Shakespeare's *Henry IV* (see "D") "Doomsday is near. Die all, die merrily."

"Where shall I begin, please your Majesty?" he asked.
"Begin at the beginning," the King said, very gravely, "and go on till you come to the end: then stop."

—Lewis Carroll,
from *Alice's Adventures in Wonderland*

A

AFTERLIFE

My kingdom is not of this world.

—Jesus, in John 18:36

We maintain that after life has passed away thou still remainst in existence, and lookest forward to the day of judgment, and according to thy deserts are assigned to misery or bliss.

—Tertullian, from The Testimony of the Christian Soul

Well, when I had been dead about thirty years, I begun to get a little anxious.

—Mark Twain, from Extract from
Captain Stormfield's Visit to Heaven

The end is where we start from.

—T. S. Eliot, from Little Gidding

CLOV: Do you believe in the life to come?
HAMM: Mine was always that.

—Samuel Beckett, from *Endgame*

One world at a time.

—Henry David Thoreau, on being asked his opinion
of the hereafter

. . . . .

AGING

Ask a woman who bears children, and she will tell you. . . .
Those born in the strength of youth are different from those born
during the time of old age, when the womb is failing. Therefore
you also should consider that you and your contemporaries are
smaller in stature than those who were before you, and those who
come after you will be smaller than you, as born of a creation that
already is aging and passing the strength of youth.

—2 Esdras 5:51–55

Alas for these latter days! The world had grown old, and all its
inmates partook of the decrepitude. Why talk of infancy, man-
hood, and old age? We all stood equal sharers of the last throes
of time-worn nature.

—Mary Shelley, from *The Last Man*

. . . . .

AIDS

After we tested [HIV] positive, we became kleptomaniacs. . . .
Ours was a typical American response to the threat of death, the
loss of meaning. . . . We're dignified now. . . . Still I get testy: I've
been promised the end of the world since I was a kid; it's my
Christian apocalyptic heritage, and I'm hoping I won't be disappointed. Please, everything burst. . . . We want to kiss serpents
and explode into fragments in one final, glorious moment.

—Stephen Beachy, from *Next: Young American Writers
on the New Generation*

I hope I didn't give you AIDS! . . . Oh, merely jesting! Mind
you I think AIDS is rather healthy in its way. It's not a fashion-
able thing to say, but the world is overcrowded, isn't it? It could
do with a bit of pruning.

—from *Naked*,
film written and directed by Mike Leigh

By the year 2000, about 12 percent of Kenyans will have HIV.
In Lusaka, Zambia, cemeteries are running out of space to bury
the dead.

—from *Newsweek*, Dec. 12, 1994

. . . . .

ANARCHY

This condition, a close cousin of Chaos, is often interpreted as one of the significant signs of the approaching End.

> Turning and turning in the widening gyre
> The falcon cannot hear the falconer;
> Things fall apart; the centre cannot hold;
> Mere anarchy is loosed upon the world.

— William Butler Yeats, from "The Second Coming"

My fellow Americans, we live in an age of anarchy, both abroad and at home.

— Richard M. Nixon, TV address on incursion into
Cambodia, April 30, 1970

. . . . .

ANGELS

Characters frequently appearing in apocalypses (it is often useful to think of an apocalypse as an ancient popular literary form), angels become the channel or source of the revelation. In particular, one should be on guard and alert if the angels/messengers appear in gangs and bear instruments such as trumpets, vials, seals, or scrolls, as per the havoc wreaked by the seven angels of Revelation, whose damage report is abridged:

The *first* angel blew his trumpet, and a third of the earth was burned up. The *second* angel blew his, and a third of the sea became blood. The *third* angel, and a blazing star called Wormwood [which is poison] fell from heaven. The *fourth* angel, and the light of the sun, moon, and stars was darkened. The *fifth* angel blew his and locusts equipped like horses in battle dress emerged from the earth. When the *sixth* angel blew, a cavalry of two hundred million horses breathing sulfur killed another third of humankind. The *seventh* and final angel appeared bestriding sea and land, and bearing a scroll, and was about to do in the rest of evil mankind with seven thunders, but his hand was stayed, for he will blow his trumpet only when the mystery of God is fulfilled. . . .

—from Revelation 8–10

In heaven an angel is nobody in particular.

—George Bernard Shaw, from *Man and Superman*

Well, angels have to go to the earth every day—millions of them—to appear in visions to dying children and good people, you know—it's the heft of their business.

—Mark Twain, from *Extract from Captain Stormfield's Visit to Heaven*

. . . . .

ANTICHRIST

The legendary antagonist and deviously evil counterpart—the anti—of the returned Christ in the last great cosmic battles, whose culmination in the Christian tradition ushers in the end of the world. Final Enemy, Evil One, Final Adversary, and Destroyer are among his numerous aliases, because Deceit is a big part of his game. Antichrist historically has been a catchall for just about anybody you don't like, from persecuting Roman emperors to popes to presidents. Through the more sophisticated interpretations of thinkers such as St. Augustine, Antichrist has also been spiritualized to refer less to an external enemy and more to thoughts and behaviors that are unchristian within each human heart. The Final Adversary is conceived of as the apogee of evil. He is always a human agent—as opposed to the nonhuman Devil—and he is one of the great leitmotifs of apocalyptic thinking, although in modern times the daunting dung-bearded guy who formerly terrified generations has dwindled largely into metaphor.

Children, it is the last hour! As you have heard that antichrist is coming, so now many antichrists have come. From this we know that it is the last hour.

—1 John 2:18

I feel much freer now that I am certain the Pope is Antichrist.

—Martin Luther

As distinct from other forms of conservative religion, fundamentalism requires confrontation and opposition. It requires a worthy adversary. . . . The story of the 20th-century Antichrist is largely the story of naming, dramatizing, and mythologizing the enemies of ultra-conservative Protestantism.

—Robert Fuller, from *Naming the Antichrist*

The church is always in danger of becoming Anti-Christ because it is not sufficiently eschatological. It lives too little by faith and hope and too much by the pretensions of its righteousness.

—Reinhold Niebuhr, from "The Church and the End of History"

Why do I think McDonald's is the Antichrist?

—Bill Hicks, comedian, Dominion Theater, London, 1993

. . . . .

ANTINOMIANISM

The destabilizing doctrine that when the messiah arrives, or when the extreme imminence of the final redemptive times is declared by the messiah's prophets, conventional behavior and law—even the Ten Commandments—no longer apply; the forbidden is therefore permissible, even encouraged as a kind of public demonstration of one's belief in the transformative powers of redemption. Among the most notable antinomian outbreaks have been the takeover of the German city of Münster by radical Anabaptists led by Jan Bockelson in 1535, the Frankist movement among the Jews of seventeenth-century Poland, and the Millerites in America in 1843–44. Usually fueled by the megalomania of a charismatic leader, newly encouraged activities included the abolition of private property, the selling off of all one's earthly possessions, public nudity, and polygamy.

Praise be to Thee, O Lord, who permittest the forbidden.

—blasphemous benediction ascribed to the Frankists (followers of Jacob Frank), radical followers of Sabbatai Zevi, from *Major Trends in Jewish Mysticism* by Gerschom Scholem

Assured that every transgression was a rung in the ladder of self-purification and spiritual elevation, the people of Goray sank to the forty-nine Gates of Impurity. . . . Reb Gedalia was said to have secreted a whore. . . . A copper cross hung on his breast. . . . God's name was everywhere desecrated.

—Isaac Bashevis Singer, from *Satan in Goray*

Now I am given power over all nations of the earth, and the right to use the sword to the confusion of the wicked, and in defense of the righteous. So let none in this town stain himself with crime or resist the will of God, or else he without delay shall be put to death with the sword. . . . My kingdom which begins now shall endure and know no downfall.

—Jan Bockelson, after being proclaimed King of the New Jerusalem of Münster

. . . . .

ANTIOCHUS (IV) EPIPHANES

Psychologically unstable ("epiphanes" means "mad") ruler of Syria in second century B.C.E., he forbade Jewish religious practice, triggering the Hasmonean/Maccabean revolt, becoming the evil protagonist of the Hanukkah story and an early prototype for Antichrist. In all likelihood, the cruelty of his rule was the impetus for the writing of the book of Daniel, perhaps the greatest Jewish apocalyptic source book (and the only full-fledged apocalypse in the Hebrew Bible) as well as the key inspiration for the primary Christian apocalyptic text, Revelation. In all likelihood Antiochus is the famous and horrible talking "little horn" of Daniel's vision.

I was considering the horns, when another horn appeared, a little one coming up among them; to make room for it, three of the earlier horns were plucked up by the roots. There were eyes like human eyes in this horn, and a mouth speaking arrogantly.

—Daniel 7:8

The times of Antichrist will be necessarily deadly, like the times when Antiochus tried to make people commit apostasy under his reign. The Antichrist will attempt to do what Antiochus could not, since he had not the time.

—Quintus Julius Hilarianus, from *The Progress of Time*, Bernard McGinn, trans.

. . . . .

APOCALYPSE

From the Greek words apo *("from") and* kalyptein *("to cover")— thus "uncover"—refers to a disclosure or revelation usually via a prophet, angel, or other mysterious messenger. While not every revelation—the Ten Commandments, for example—is an apocalypse, most apocalyptic messages preview group, national, or universal fate, and very often the ultimate and final disposition of humankind and the world—End Times. While the word "apocalypse" was used as late as Samuel Johnson's eighteenth-century dictionary "only in relation to the sacred writings," over time the term has been expanded and secularized so that, at risk of losing its original momentous and moral force, it now is employed in reference to fundamental political and cultural changes that arrive with a jolting, violent, surprising power.*

Surely the Lord God does nothing,
without revealing his secret to his servants the prophets.
The lion has roared; who will not fear?
The Lord God has spoken; who can but prophesy?

—Amos 3:7–8

If God is to speak his word to the world, it must be still and at peace.

—Meister Eckhart, from *Sermons*

Instead of complaining that God had hidden himself, you will give him thanks for having revealed so much of himself.

—Blaise Pascal, from *Pensées*

The Torah releases one word, and comes forth from her sheath ever so little, and then retreats to concealment again.

—from "Lovers of the Torah," in the *Zohar*

It was subtle of God to learn Greek when he wished to become an author—and not learn it better.

—Friedrich Nietzsche, from *Beyond Good and Evil*

Even before it finally banned all apocalypses, Judaism must have been suspicious of them because of their wildness of fantasy, their waywardness and randomness, as well as their overemphasis on eschatology. Prophetic and Rabbinic Judaism was predominantly interested in the progress of man and society, while the apocalypses were interested in the timetable of the approaching End.

—Abba Hillel Silver, from *Where Judaism Differs*

Apocalypse can be disconfirmed without being discredited. This is part of its extraordinary resilience.

—Frank Kermode, from *The Sense of an Ending:
Studies in the Theory of Fiction*

If God has spoken, why is the universe not convinced?

—Percy Bysshe Shelley, from *Queen Mab*

The vast bulk of the population believe that morality depends entirely on revelation; and if a doubt could be raised . . . men would think they were at liberty to steal, and women would consider themselves absolved from the restraints of chastity.

—John Campbell, from *Argument for the prosecution
in* Rex. v. H. Hetherington

. . . . .

ARMAGEDDON

The ultimate battleground, as forecast in Revelation, where Jesus will destroy the last evil armies thrown against him. Its specific location was probably in the environs of the ancient fortress of Megiddo—from which Armageddon is etymologically derived—on the Plain of Jezreel in northern Israel.

I sometimes believe we're heading very fast for Armageddon right now.

—Ronald Reagan, quoted in the *Boston Globe*,
May 2, 1982

Armageddon: All lands in play are to be destroyed.

—instructions from Magic: The Gathering,
children's card game

I did not feel Armageddon in my bones but I worried about all those people who did, who were ready for it, wishing hard, making phone calls and bank withdrawals. If enough people want it to happen, will it happen? How many people are enough?

—Don DeLillo, from *White Noise*

Señor, señor, do you know where we're headin'?
Lincoln County Road or Armageddon?

—Bob Dylan, from "Señor (Tales of Yankee Power)"

I saw three foul spirits . . . from the mouth of the dragon, from the mouth of the beast, and from the mouth of the false prophet . . . who go abroad to the kings of the whole world, to assemble them for battle on the great day of God the Almighty. . . . And they assembled them at the place that in Hebrew is called Harmagedon. . . . And there came flashes of lightning, rumblings, peals of thunder, and a violent earthquake, such as had not occurred since people were upon the earth.

—Revelation 16:13–18

. . . . .

ART AND ARCHITECTURE

We come from a world where we have known incredible standards of excellence, and we dimly remember beauties which we have not seized again. . . . The public for which masterpieces are intended is not on this earth.

— Thornton Wilder, from *The Bridge of San Luis Rey*

I Sandro painted this picture at the end of the year 1500 in the troubles of Italy in the half time after the time according to the eleventh chapter of Saint John in the second woe of the Apocalypse in the loosing of the devil for three and a half years. Then he will be chained in the twelfth chapter and we shall see him trodden down as in this picture.

— inscription at top of Botticelli's painting of the Nativity, Florence

So long as the system of competition in the production and exchange of the means of life goes on, the degradation of the arts will go on; and if that system is to last forever, then art is doomed, and will surely die; that is to say, civilization will die.

— William Morris, from *Art Under Plutocracy*

We shall not have succeeded in demolishing everything unless we demolish the ruins as well. But the only way I can see of doing that is to use them to put up a lot of fine, well-designed buildings.

— Alfred Jarry, from *Ubu Enchained*

The art and art-polemics of this century have been so often beset with the sweats and chills of apocalyptic yearning that some have seen modernism as that product of Western history that tries to self-destruct, taking history with it.

—Carter Ratcliff, from "Narrative," in
The Print Collector's Newsletter Jan./Feb. 1982

Great is the art of beginning, but greater is the art of ending.

—Henry Wadsworth Longfellow

. . . . .

ASTEROIDS

The world ended Sunday night—at least on CBS. *Without Warning*, a TV movie filmed as a breaking news broadcast, covered the crash of asteroids into Earth. CBS aired disclaimers, but many viewers still were convinced the sky was falling: In Sacramento, callers to KXTV got a recording, "None of what you are seeing is actually happening." WUSA, in Washington, D.C., took about one hundred calls. "Some people were mad when they found out it wasn't true," said Tony Williams of WUSA.

—Gary Fields and Leo Mullen, in *U.S.A. Today*,
Nov. 1, 1994

There is a growing body of evidence that the earth has indeed been hit frequently by asteroids and comets. That we are, quite simply, a sitting duck for disasters. . . . Some scientists argue that at least one impact of a celestial body accompanied four of the five major [species] extinctions over the past 100 million years.

—Charles Panati, from *Panati's Extraordinary Endings*

. . . . .

Atomic and Hydrogen Bombs

I am become death, the destroyer of worlds.

—J. Robert Oppenheimer

As the bomb fell over Hiroshima and exploded, we saw an entire city disappear. I wrote in my log the words: "My God, what have we done?"

—Captain Robert Lewis, from comments on 10th anniversary of first nuclear bomb

. . . . .

Aum Shinrikyo ("Supreme Truth") The Japanese "Doomsday" Cult

As we move toward the year 2000, there will be a series of events of inexpressible ferocity and terror. . . . The lands of Japan will be transformed into a nuclear wasteland. Between 1996 and January 1998 America and its allies will attack Japan, and only 10% of the population of the major cities will survive.

—text from Aum Shinrikyo booklet

. . . . .

Aviation

One of these nights about twelve o'clock
The old world's going to reel and rock

The sinner's going to tremble and cry for pain
And the Lord will come in his aeroplane.

O ye thirsty of every tribe
Get your ticket for an aeroplane ride,
Jesus our Savior is a-coming to reign
And take you up to glory in His aeroplane.

—Anonymous, from "The Heavenly Aeroplane,"
folk song

B

BABYLON

This is the harlot-ridden city from whose sinful depths Antichrist allegedly hails. Identification with Babylon became the great all-purpose municipal and moral smear for Rome, then, in the Middle Ages, for the seat of the false pope, false and corrupt church, centers of luxury and decadence—usually the greatest cities in the world—and, over time, the extreme indicting curse for just about any locale you want to slur and defame.

And Babylon, the glory of kingdoms . . . will be like Sodom and Gomorrah . . . It will never be inhabited or lived in for all generations. . . . Wild animals will lie down there, and its houses will be full of howling creatures. . . . Hyenas will cry in its towers, and jackals in the pleasant palaces.

—Isaiah 13:19–22

The woman was clothed in purple and scarlet, and adorned with gold and jewels and pearls, holding in her hand a golden cup full of abominations and the impurities of her fornication; and on her forehead was written a name, a mystery: "Babylon, the great, mother of whores and of earth's abominations." And I saw that the woman was drunk with the blood of the saints and the blood of the witnesses to Jesus.

—Revelation 17:4–6

. . . . .

BEASTS

Among the most graphic creations of the early apocalyptists, beasts are protean poetic collages of traits and thunderous talents and powers almost always in the service of evil. Apocalyptic animals enable the writers to have it both ways—to be both mythical and topical—and thus come up with creations that are often symbolic of the group's enemies. These have ranged from Antiochus and the Syrians to Nero and the Romans. The ultimate beast is identified with Satan, and Revelation gives him a secret number, 666, about which much ado has been made—particularly by contemporary American prophecy-marketeers—from street addresses to avoid to a conspiracy based on the universal bar code.

I, Daniel, saw in my vision by night the four winds of heaven stirring up the great sea, and four great beasts came up out of the sea, different from one another. The first was like a lion and had eagle wings . . . and a human mind was given to it. . . . Another . . . looked like a bear . . . another appeared, like a leopard . . . a fourth beast . . . was different from all the beasts that preceded it, and it had ten horns.

—Daniel 7:2–7

And I saw a beast rising out of the sea. . . . One of its heads seemed to have received a death-blow, but its mortal wound had been healed. In amazement the whole earth followed the beast. . . . Then I saw another beast that rose out of the earth; it had two horns like a lamb and it spoke like a dragon . . . it deceives the inhabitants of earth. . . . Also it causes all . . . to be marked on the right hand or the forehead. . . . Its number is six hundred sixty-six.

—Revelation 13

God lay dead in heaven;
Angels sang the hymn of the end. . . .
But of all sadness this was sad—
A woman's arms tried to shield
The head of a sleeping man
From the jaws of the final beast.

—Stephen Crane

Surely some revelation is at hand;
. . . A shape with lion body and the head of a man,
A gaze blank and pitiless as the sun,
Is moving its slow thighs, while all about it
Reel shadows of the indignant desert birds.
The darkness drops again; but now I know
That twenty centuries of stony sleep

Were vexed to nightmare by a rocking cradle,
And what rough beast, its hour come round at last,
Slouches towards Bethlehem to be born?

—William Butler Yeats, from "The Second Coming"

Wild dark times are rumbling toward us, and the prophet who wishes to write a new apocalypse will have to invent entirely new beasts, and beasts so terrible that the ancient animal symbols of St. John will seem like cooing doves and cupids in comparison.

—Heinrich Heine

. . . . .

BELIEF

To believe in signs and wonders . . . in gods and devils, in heavens and hells, makes the brain an insane ward, the world a madhouse . . . destroys the kinship of effect and cause. . . . Nature becomes a puppet of unseen powers.

—Robert Ingersoll

It is our task in the world to believe things no one else takes seriously. To abandon such beliefs completely, the human race would die. This is why we are here. A tiny minority. To embody old things, old beliefs. The devil, the angels, heaven, hell. If we did not pretend to believe these things, the world would collapse.

—Don DeLillo, from *White Noise*

. . . . .

BIOLOGY

The biological destruction of mankind would, of course, be the end of the world in a stricter sense. As for the destruction of all life on the planet, it would be not merely a human but a planetary end—the death of the earth. And although the annihilation of other forms of life could hardly be of concern to human beings once they themselves had been annihilated, this more comprehensive, planetary termination is nevertheless full of sorrowful meaning for us as we reflect on the possibility now, while we still exist.

—Jonathan Schell, from *The Fate of the Earth*

. . . . . .

BOOKS

There are signs that the world is speedily coming to an end: Bribery and corruption are common. Children no longer obey their parents, and everyone is writing a book [probably a last will and testament, as opposed to a best-seller!].

—from Assyrian tablet, 2800 B.C.E.

I, John, your brother who share with you in Jesus the persecution and the kingdom and the patient endurance . . . was in the spirit on the Lord's day, and I heard behind me a loud voice like a trumpet saying, "Write in a book what you see and send it to the seven churches, to Ephesus, to Smyrna, to Pergamum, to Thyatira, to Sardis, to Philadelphia, and to Laodicea."

—Revelation 1:9–11

When the seal is placed upon the age that is about to pass away, then I will show these signs: the books shall be opened before the face of the firmament, and all shall see my judgment together.

—2 Esdras 6:20

. . . . .

BRANCH DAVIDIANS

When we joined, David was planning to lead the group to Israel to retake Jerusalem. He taught that there would be a big battle between the forces of the world and David and his people. The world would win, and we would be killed, but we would come back in a cloud and smite the wicked and retake the world. . . . There never was a time when we didn't expect to be killed by the feds.

—Kiri Jewell, who lived at the Waco compound until shortly before the raid

. . . . .

BROOKLYN BRIDGE

If
the end of the world
                befall
and chaos
    smash our planet
                    to bits,
and what remains
                will be
                    this
bridge, rearing above the dust of destruction;
then,
    as huge ancient lizards
                    are rebuilt
from bones
        finer than needles,
                        to tower in museums,
so,
    from this bridge,
                a geologist of the centuries
will succeed
            in re-creating
                        our contemporary world.

— Vladimir Mayakovsky, from "Brooklyn Bridge"

. . . . .

BUDDHISM

When the many are reduced to one, to what is the One reduced?

> —Zen (Buddhist) koan, from *The Little Zen Companion*, David Schiller, ed.

A monk asked old Abbot Ch'iu-Ch'iu, "When the firestorm at the end of the world sweeps through, and everything is burned up, does the Buddha Nature burn with it?"

"Hand me a light," said Ch'iu-Ch'iu.

The student touched a taper to the charcoal footwarmer and gave it to him. Ch'iu-Ch'iu set the student's robe on fire, then yelled, "Put it out! Put it out!"

Concerning this case, Brother Pseudo comments:

> By firelight the patchrobe monk puts his question,
> Yet he sees not the blazes all about him
> When did the world end for him!
> Wasn't it only yesterday?
> Bah! His farts add fuel to the fire!

> —from "The Yellow Cliff Record," quoted in *Beyond Armageddon*, Walter M. Miller, Jr., ed.

. . . . .

BUDGETING

Due to cutbacks the light at the end of the tunnel will be turned off.

> —sign hanging in office at Mt. Sinai Hospital (pediatric cardiology), New York, 1995

. . . . .

BUSY SIGNAL

God seems to have left the receiver off the hook, and time is running out.

—Arthur Koestler, from *The Ghost in the Machine*

C

CALCULATORS

For the day of the Lord is as a thousand years; and in six days created things were finished; it is evident, therefore, that they will come to an end in the six thousandth year.

—Iraneus, from *Against Heresy*

In vain, then, do we attempt to compute definitely the years that may remain to this world. . . . Yet some have said that four hundred, some five hundred, others a thousand years, may be completed from the ascension of the Lord up to His final coming. But on this subject He puts aside the figures of the calculators and orders silence and says, "It is not for you to know the times, which the Father hath put in His own power."

—St. Augustine, from *City of God*

Taken together, the mass density and the Hubble Constant— a measure of the universe's rate of expansion, some 40 to 100 kilometers per second per megaparsec, a parsec being 3.26 light-years—tell us whether the universe will expand forever in the "big chill" or collapse one day in the "big squeeze." There is no doubt that these are profound numbers. Our understanding of the fate of the universe rests upon them.

—Neil de Grasse Tyson, from *Natural History* magazine, Feb. 1995

The world as we know it is being destroyed. Sorry, but it's the truth. In a short time—I don't know—in three years, maybe five years, could be ten years, I don't know, there's gonna be war. It's gonna be called the War of Armageddon . . . as sure as you are standing there, it's gonna happen.

—Bob Dylan, quoted in *in his own words*, Christian Williams, ed.

Blasted be the bones of those who calculate the end, for when the calculated time comes and Messiah does not appear, people despair of his ever coming.

—Rabbi Jonathan, from *Talmud: Sanhedrin*

. . . . .

CALIFORNIA

Words, pictures, numbers, facts, graphics, statistics, specks, waves, particles, motes. Only a catastrophe gets our attention. We want them, we need them, we depend on them. As long as they happen somewhere else. This is where California comes in. Mud slides, brush fires, coastal erosion, earthquakes, mass killings, et cetera. We can relax and enjoy these disasters because in our hearts we feel that California deserves whatever it gets. Californians invented the concept of life-style. This alone warrants their doom.

—Don DeLillo, from *White Noise*

. . . . .

CATS

Operationally, God is beginning to resemble not a ruler but the last fading smile of a cosmic Cheshire cat.

—Sir Julian Huxley, from *Religion Without Revelation*

. . . . .

CHAOS

Chaos is the score upon which reality is written.

—Henry Miller, from *Tropic of Cancer*

The present world chaos is not just by chance. We have arrived at the hour of apocalypse.

—Luc Jouret, leader of the Order of the Solar Temple

There shall be chaos also in many places, fire shall often break out, the wild animals shall roam beyond their haunts, and menstruous women shall bring forth monsters.

—2 Esdras 5:8

Lo! thy dread Empire Chaos! is restored;
Light dies before thy uncreating word:
Thy hand, great Anarch! lets the curtain fall;
And universal Darkness buries All.

—Alexander Pope, from *The Dunciad*

. . . . .

CHOICE

The point was that there were people who could destroy mankind and that they were foolish and arrogant, crazy, and must be begged not to do it. Let the enemies of life step down. Let each man now examine his heart. Without a great change of heart, I would not trust myself in a position of authority. Do I love mankind? Enough to spare it, if I should be in a position to blow it to hell?

—Saul Bellow, from *Herzog*

We have one foot in genesis and the other in apocalypse, and annihilation is always one immediate option.

—Michael Harrington, from *Toward a Democratic Left*

I decline to accept the end of man.

—William Faulkner,
in his Nobel Prize acceptance speech

There is a terrible urge to kill, murder, and destroy in people. Unless there is a complete metamorphosis in people, everything that has been built up will be destroyed.

—Anne Frank

. . . . .

CITIES

Was there ever a metropolis—apart perhaps from Jerusalem—that has been considered a healthy and spiritually positive place to spend one's days? Berated by Jeremiah, Amos, and just about everyone, secular and ecclesiastical, who has followed, cities are the headquarters of corruption and evil (Antichrist himself allegedly hails from Babylon) and they are therefore No. 1 on Destruction's hit parade.

There was no large city with a vaster torment we might use to see our own dilemma in some soothing perspective. No large city to blame for our sense of victimization. No city to hate and fear. No panting megacenter to absorb our woe. . . .

—Don DeLillo, from *White Noise*

Hell was the ultimate inner city. Its stinking sulfurous streets were unsafe. Everywhere Ellerbee looked he saw atrocities. . . . Everything was contagious, cancer as common as a cold, plague the quotidian. . . . Nerves like a hideous body hair grew long enough to trip over and lay raw and exposed as live wires or shoelaces that had come undone.

—Stanley Elkin, from *The Living End*

. . . . .

CIVIC RELIGION

Like virtually all other Judeo-Christian religions, the American civic religion made eschatological predictions: It promised a utopian future to believers in the end of days. And then an amazing thing happened—a thing without parallel, so far as I know, in the whole history of religion: In the years following the Second World War, those utopian promises came true.

—David Gelernter, from *1939: The Lost World of the Fair*

There's only one person who ever lived who I would trust to impose values on America. And when He comes back, He won't need government to impose His values.

—Phil Gramm, speaking at the Christian Coalition convention Oct. 9, 1995

. . . . .

CIVILIZATION

It is impossible to maintain a civilization with twelve-year-olds having babies, fifteen-year-olds killing each other, seventeen-year-olds dying of AIDS, and eighteen-year-olds getting diplomas they can't read. . . .

We're at the edge of losing this civilization. You get two more generations of what we've had for the last twenty years and we're in desperate trouble.

> —Newt Gingrich, the *New York Times* and
> the *Atlanta Journal*, 1994

The end of the human race will be that it will eventually die of civilization.

> —Ralph Waldo Emerson, from *Essays*

It is time for man to make a new appraisal of himself. His failure is abject. His plans for the future are infantile. The varied forms of his civilization in this century are smashing each other.

> —Philip Wylie, from *Generation of Vipers*

You can't say civilization don't advance, however, for in every war they kill you in a new way.

> —Will Rogers, in *Autobiography of Will Rogers*,
> Donald Daye, ed.

. . . . .

COCKROACH

The insect distinctively bound up with 20th-century civilization has been the cockroach. . . . Cockroaches appeared on Earth during the Carboniferous Age, some 320,000,000 years ago, and they may be the final denizens of a planet carbonized by nuclear explosions.

—Hillel Schwartz, from *Century's End*

. . . . .

COLLEGE EDUCATION

You may have your college education to hang on to now, but you're gonna need something very solid to hang on to when these [end] days come.

—Bob Dylan, quoted in *in his own words*,
Christian Williams, ed.

. . . . .

COLUMBUS, CHRISTOPHER

Columbus noted in the diary of his first voyage, in 1492, that his great adventure began precisely on the day the Jews were expelled from Spain. A man of his time and mystical interests would certainly have known and felt the significant Christian symbolism of this synchronicity: that the Jews' return to the Holy Land, the rebuilding of the Temple, and then their conversion to the true faith were necessary, prophesied steps to the End. Expulsion did not, of course, mean that the irritatingly enduring Jewish people would flee to the Moslem-dominated Holy Land. Yet in his deeply spiritual heart Columbus must have experienced a rush of feeling that cried out to him: Ah, it begins!

God made me the messenger of the new heaven and the new earth of which he spoke in the Apocalypse of St. John after having spoken of it through the mouth of Isaiah: and he showed me the spot where to find it.

—Christopher Columbus

. . . . .

COMPUTERS

I do not worry much about the computers that are wired to help me find a friend among fifty thousand. If errors are made, I can always beg off with a headache. But what of the vaster machines that will be giving instructions to cities, to nations? If they are programmed to regulate human behavior according to today's view of nature, we are surely in for apocalypse.

—Lewis Thomas, from "An Earnest Proposal," in *The Lives of a Cell*

My impression is that the Doomsday Models divert attention from remedial public policy by permitting everyone to blame "the predicament of mankind." Who could pay attention to a humdrum affair like legislation to tax sulfur emissions when the date of the Apocalypse has just been announced by a computer?

—Robert M. Solow

. . . . .

CONFUSION

And the sun shall suddenly begin
   to shine at night,
     and the moon during the day.
Blood shall drip from wood,
   and the stone shall utter its voice;
the peoples shall be troubled,
   and the stars shall fall.

—2 Esdras 5:4–5

Oh, what did you see, my blue-eyed son?
Oh, what did you see my darling young one?
I saw a newborn baby with wild wolves all around it,
I saw a highway of diamonds with nobody on it,
I saw a black branch with blood that kept drippin',
I saw a room full of men with their hammers a-bleedin',
I saw a white ladder all covered with water,
I saw ten thousand talkers whose tongues were all broken,
I saw guns and sharp swords in the hands of young children,
And it's a hard, and it's a hard, it's a hard, it's a hard,
And it's a hard rain a-gonna fall.

—Bob Dylan, from "A Hard Rain's A-Gonna Fall"

. . . . .

Congress

One of the Lincoln stories has it that, during his 1846 campaign, he attended a preaching service of Peter Cartwright. The evangelist called on all who wished to go to Heaven to stand up. All rose but Lincoln. The evangelist called for all to rise who did not want to go to Hell. "I am grieved," said Cartwright, "to see Abe Lincoln sitting back there unmoved by these appeals. If he doesn't want to go to Heaven and doesn't want to escape Hell, will he tell us where he does want to go?"

Lincoln got up slowly and said, "I am going to Congress."

—from *2500 Anecdotes for All Occasions*, E. Fuller, ed.

Due to the lack of experienced trumpeters, the End of the World has been postponed for three weeks!

—sign hung on the chamber of Rules Committee,
U.S. House of Representatives, 1970

. . . . .

Consciousness

The world begins and ends with us. Only our consciousness exists, it is everything, and this everything vanishes with it.

—E. M. Cioran, from *Anathemas and Admirations*

How can he exalt his thoughts to anything great and noble who only believes that, after a short turn on the stage of this world, he is to sink into oblivion, and to lose his consciousness forever?

—John Hughes, from *The Spectator*

. . . . .

COUNTER CULTURE

Many uneasy intellectuals . . . fear that the counter culture arrives, not trailing clouds of glory, but bearing the mark of the beast. No sooner does one speak of liberating the non-intellective powers of the personality than, for many, a prospect of the starkest character arises: a vision of rampant, antinomian mania, which in the name of permissiveness threatens to plunge us into a dark and savage age.

—Theodore Roszak, from *The Making of a Counter Culture*

. . . . .

CREATIVITY

The urge for destruction is also a creative urge!

—Mikhail Bakunin

Even our power of destruction is hardly our own. . . . Nuclear energy was nature's creation, and was only discovered by us. . . . Our modest role is not to create but only to preserve ourselves. The alternative is to surrender ourselves to absolute and eternal darkness: a darkness in which . . . never again will human beings appear on the earth, and there will be no one to remember that they ever did.

—Jonathan Schell, from *The Fate of the Earth*

. . . . .

CRUSADES

A strange idea had taken possession of the popular mind at the close of the tenth and commencement of the eleventh century. It was universally believed that the end of the world was at hand; that the thousand years of the Apocalypse were near completion, and that Jesus Christ would descend upon Jerusalem to judge mankind. All Christendom was in commotion. . . . Forsaking their homes, kindred, and occupation, they crowded to Jerusalem to await the coming of the Lord, lightened, as they imagined, of a load of sin by their weary pilgrimage.

—Charles Mackay, from *Extraordinary Popular
Delusions and the Madness of Crowds*

. . . . .

CUBAN MISSILE CRISIS

Seven thousand megatons would also have been more than enough fire and brimstone to initiate a lethal nuclear winter over at least the Northern Hemisphere, freezing and starving yet more millions in Europe, Asia, and North America. If John Kennedy had followed LeMay's advice, history would have forgotten the Nazis and their terrible Holocaust. Ours would have been the historic omnicide.

—Richard Rhodes, from "The General and World War
III," in *The New Yorker*, June 19, 1995

. . . . .

CULTURE

If Christianity goes, the whole of our culture goes. Then you must start painfully again, and you cannot put on a new culture ready made. You must wait for the grass to grow to feed the sheep to give the wool out of which your new coat will be made. You must pass through many centuries of barbarism.

—T. S. Eliot, in "Notes Towards the Definition of Culture"

The destruction of human civilization, even without the biological destruction of the human species, may perhaps rightly be called the end of the world, since it would be the end of that sum of cultural achievements and human relationships which constitutes what many people mean when they speak of "the world."

—Jonathan Schell, from *The Fate of the Earth*

I miss the fear of nuclear obliteration; at least it promised a quick end. Now, with a handful of God-given exceptions, the culture howls through eternity like Marley's ghost—stupid, lazy, boring—and audiences love every minute!

—Roger Rosenblatt, from "New York Diarist," in *The New Republic*, Feb. 20, 1995

D

DAY OF JUDGMENT

And I saw the dead, great and small, standing before the throne, and books were opened. Also another book was opened, the book of life. And the dead were judged according to their works, as recorded in the books. And the sea gave up the dead that were in it, Death and Hades gave up the dead that were in them, and all were judged according to what they had done.

—Revelation 20:12–13

Only our concept of time makes it possible for us to speak of the Day of Judgment; in reality it is a constant court in perpetual session.

—Franz Kafka

For my part I am sure that the Day of Judgment is just around the corner. It doesn't matter that we don't know the precise day . . . perhaps someone else can figure it out. But it is certain that time is now at an end.

—Martin Luther

> The aged earth aghast
> With terror of that blast
>   Shall from the surface to the center shake,
> When, at the world's last session,
> The dreadful Judge in middle air shall spread
>   His throne.

—John Milton, from "On the Morning of
Christ's Nativity"

> You who in different sects have shammed,
> And come to see each other damned;
> (So some folks told you, but they knew
> No more of Jove's designs than you)
> The World's mad business now is o'er,
> And I resent these pranks no more.
> I to such blockheads set my wit!
> I damn such fools! Go, go, you're bit.

—Jonathan Swift, from "The Day of Judgment"

. . . . .

DAY OF THE LORD

A very old Biblical idea, referring to an eschatalogical, terror-filled settling of the score between a frustrated, angry God and man—a precursor to Christian notions of the Day of Judgment. While the Jewish precedent, created in the prophetic tradition, is generally limited to threatened destruction of a wayward Israel or its enemies as a corrective step for future improved behavior here on earth, the Christian innovation is a far more universal wipeout and echoes, perhaps, the earlier mythical obliterations such as flood stories.

> The great day of the Lord is near,
> near and hastening fast . . .
> I will bring such distress upon people
> that they shall walk like the blind . . .
> Neither their silver nor their gold
> will be able to save them
> on the day of the Lord's wrath;
> in the fire of his passion
> the whole earth shall be consumed;
> for a full, terrible end
> he will make of all the
> inhabitants of the earth.
>
> —Zephaniah 1:14–18

> Ah! what terror shall be shaping
> When the Judge the truth's undraping—
> Cats from every bag escaping!
>
> . . . When thy sheep thou has selected
> From the goats, may I, respected,
> Stand amongst them undetected.

On that day of lamentation,
When, to enjoy the conflagration,
Men come forth, O be not cruel:
Spare me, Lord—make them thy fuel.

—Ambrose Bierce, from "The Day of Wrath"

. . . . .

DEATH WISH

The goal of all life is death.

—Sigmund Freud, quoted in the *New York Times*,
May 6, 1956

Thou has conquered, O Pale Galilean; the world
grown grey from thy breath;
We have drunken of things Lethean, and fed on the
fullness of death.

—Algernon Charles Swinburne, from
"Hymn to Proserpine"

The most disquieting psychological feature of our time, and the one which affords the best argument for the necessity of some creed, however irrational, is the death wish. . . . There is a tendency to shrug the shoulders and say, "Oh well, if we are exterminated by hydrogen bombs, it will save a lot of trouble. . . ." It can only be met by courage, hope, and a reasoned optimism.

—Bertrand Russell, from *The Impact of Science
on Society*

····

DECEIT

*From the falseness of prophets to the inexhaustible and clever
ways Antichrist can fraudulently replicate the behavior of the returning Jesus—including the performing of miracles—deceit and
the need to guard against it are recurring themes in apocalyptic
literature.*

Beware of false prophets, who come to you in sheep's clothing
but inwardly are ravenous wolves.

—Matthew 7:15

The devil can cite Scripture for his purpose.

—William Shakespeare, from *The Merchant of Venice*

····

DENIAL

Today the constant presence of the cataclysm as a possibility—indeed a probability—offers a signal opportunity for reflec-
tion as such, and at the same time the one chance for the
political rebirth that would avert the cataclysm. A refusal to know
is already part of the disaster.

—Karl Jaspers, from *The Future of Mankind*

We are a civilization sunk in an unshakable commitment to
genocide, gambling madly with the universal extinction of our

species. And how viciously we ravish our sense of humanity to pretend, even for a day, that such horror can be accepted as "normal," as "necessary."

—Theodore Roszak, from *The Making of a Counter Culture*

End of Millennium
       Earth's decay—
Fire Air Water tainted
   We're the Great Beast—
       Dark bed thoughts,
Can't do anything to stop it—
Denial in Government, in Newspapers of Record—
Like watching gum disease & not brushing teeth . . .
. . . Need President who'll reverse the denial
  The Calm Panic Party
to restore nature's balance.

—Allen Ginsberg, from "Calm Panic Campaign Promise" in *Cosmopolitan Greetings*

. . . . .

DE-PEOPLED

Don't you find it a beautiful clean thought, a world empty of people, just uninterrupted grass, and a hare sitting up?

—D. H. Lawrence, from *Women in Love*

. . . . .

DEVALUATION

Our idea of human life has changed, thinned out. We can't help but think less of it now. The human race has declassed itself. It does not live anymore; it just survives, like an animal. We endure the suicide's shame, the shame of the murderer, the shame of the victim. Death is all we have in common.

—Martin Amis, from *Einstein's Monsters*

. . . . .

DEVIL

This fabled culprit is Jesus' final antagonist in the apocalyptic scenario. Only after Antichrist makes his appearance does the Devil, rising from the pit in which Jesus has imprisoned him for a thousand years, join in the evil alliance on the field of Armageddon, there to be ultimately defeated, ushering in the glorious End, with its judgment and rewards.

I believe that there is a devil, and here's Satan's agenda. First, he doesn't want anyone having kids. Secondly, if they do conceive, he wants them killed. If they're not killed through abortion, he wants them neglected or abused, physically, emotionally, sexually. Barring that, he wants to get them in some godless curriculum or setting, where their minds are filled with pollution.

—Randall Terry

I myself believe I may have found him [the Devil] in the face of Howard Stern. Who else would have tied up forty blocks of traffic on Fifth Avenue with a book signing?

—Mary Gordon, from "Bedeviling Satan," in
The Nation, June 26, 1995

It is so stupid of modern civilization to have given up believing in the devil when he is the only explanation of it.

—Ronald Knox, from *Let Dons Delight*

. . . . .

DIGNITY

You got to have a sense of dignity, even if you don't care, 'cause if you don't have that, civilization's doomed.

—Edward Albee, from *The American Dream*

. . . . .

DISSOLVING

The cloud-capp'd towers, the gorgeous palaces,
The solemn temples, the great globe itself,
Yea, all which it inherit, shall dissolve
And, like this insubstantial pageant faded
Leave not a rack behind.

—William Shakespeare, from *The Tempest*

When all the world dissolves,
And every creature shall be purified,
All place shall be hell that is not heaven.

—Christopher Marlowe, from *The Tragical History of
Doctor Faustus*

. . . . .

DOOMSDAY

Prophecies of doom are nothing new.

—Edward Teller, from *The Pursuit of Simplicity*

Doomsday is near. Die all, die merrily.

—William Shakespeare, *Henry IV, Part One*

HAMLET: What news?
ROSENCRANTZ: None, my lord, but that the world's grown
honest.
HAMLET: Then is doomsday near.

—William Shakespeare, from *Hamlet*

A thousand pounds and a bottle of hay
is all one thing at Doomsday.

—John Ray, from *English Proverbs*

No man has learned anything rightly until he knows that every day is Doomsday.

—Ralph Waldo Emerson, from *Society and Solitude*

Doomsday is the eighth day of the week.

—Stanley Kunitz, from "Foreign Affairs"

. . . . .

DRAMA

The doctrine of the Second Coming teaches us that we do not and cannot know when the world drama will end. The curtain may be rung down at any moment: say, before you have finished reading this paragraph.

—C. S. Lewis, from *The World's Last Night*

Out—are the lights—out all!
    And, over each quivering form,
The curtain, a funeral pall,
    Comes down with the rush of a storm,
And the angels, all pallid and wan,
    Uprising, unveiling affirm
That the play is the tragedy, "Man," And the
    hero the Conqueror Worm.

—Edgar Allan Poe, from *The Conqueror Worm*

For medieval people the stupendous drama of the Last Days was not a fantasy about some remote and indefinite future but a prophecy which was infallible and which at almost any given moment was felt to be on the point of fulfillment.

—Norman Cohn, from *The Pursuit of the Millennium*

Ꜫ

EARTHQUAKE

They had scarcely set foot in town when they felt the earth tremble under their feet; the sea rose in foaming masses in the port and smashed the ships. . . . Whirlwinds of flame and ashes covered the streets and squares; the houses collapsed, the roofs were thrown upon the foundations, and the foundations scattered; thirty thousand inhabitants of every age and both sexes were crushed under the ruins. Whistling and swearing, the sailor said: "There'll be something to pick up here." "What can be the sufficient reason for this phenomenon?" said Pangloss. "It is the Last Day!" cried Candide.

—Voltaire, from *Candide*, Richard Aldington, trans.

We were enveloped in night, not a moonless night or one dimmed by clouds but the darkness of a sealed room without lights. . . . Many lifted up their hands to the gods, but a great number believed that there were no more gods, and that this night was the world's last, eternal one.

—Pliny, on the eruption of Vesuvius

When comes the great earthquake, and the earth brings forth its burdens, and man says: "What is the matter with it?" That day it will tell its news, that thy Lord has prompted it.

—Koran 99:1–5

Not for me this slobbering at the feet of catastrophe; my Church fostered this civilization and if God wills that an earthquake destroy it I will at least refrain from singing hymns.

—John Fante, from "The Wrath of God," in *Dago Red*

. . . . .

EDUCATED GUESSING

The following events will come to pass, as we have learned: Elijah shall come; the Jews shall believe; Antichrist shall persecute; Christ shall judge; the dead shall rise, the good and the wicked shall be separated; the world shall be burned and renewed. All these things, we believe, shall come to pass; but how or in what order, human understanding cannot perfectly teach us, but only the experience of the events themselves. My opinion, however, is that they will happen in the order in which I have related them.

—St. Augustine, from *City of God*

. . . . .

EDUCATION

Human history becomes more and more a race between education and catastrophe.

—H. G. Wells, from *The Outline of History*

I shall know why, when time is over,
And I have ceased to wonder why;
Christ will explain each separate anguish
In the fair schoolroom of the sky.

—Emily Dickinson, from "I shall know why"

. . . . .

EMPEROR OF THE LAST DAYS

A powerful and legendary figure, based perhaps on the extraordinary career of Alexander the Great, he is associated with rulers and popes, particularly of the Middle Ages. Also known as the Last World Emperor, he is an additional endtime warrior, a kind of counterforce to Antichrist, sent to accompany Jesus as a secular military lieutenant in the final battles.

For to him God gave strength to perform
things like no previous one of all the kings.
For, first of all, cutting off the roots from three heads
mightily with a blow, he will give them to others to eat,

so that they will eat of the flesh of the parents of the impious
  king.

—*Sibylline Oracles* 5:220–224

. . . . .

END OF THE WORLD:
THE MARKETING OPPORTUNITY

And then he proceeded to unroll on the floor of the tent a
sleeping bag upon which were imprinted the twentieth and
twenty-first chapters of the Book of Revelation, recounting the
War of Gog and Magog, the Final Judgment, and the New
Jerusalem. "It's a beauty, isn't it? The holy words seep through
your skin while you're asleep and fend off the devil from entic-
ing you to commit the sins of the night."

—Tova Reich, from *The Jewish War*

. . . . .

ENDLESSNESS

That is what it shall be in the end that has no end. For what else
is our end, but to come to that realm of which there is no end?

—St. Augustine, from *City of God*

If some devil were to convince us that our dream of perpetual
immortality is no dream but a hard fact, such a shriek of despair
would go up from the human race, as no other conceivable horror could provoke. . . . What man is capable of the insane self-

conceit of believing that an eternity of himself would be tolerable even to himself?

—George Bernard Shaw, from *Parents and Children*

. . . . .

ENVIRONMENT

The struggle to save the global environment is in one way much more difficult than the struggle to vanquish Hitler, for this time the war is with ourselves. We are the enemy, just as we have only ourselves as allies. In a war such as this, then, what is victory and how will we recognize it?

—Al Gore

If we continue destroying the natural environment, which is really part of human life, we will thereby destroy any chance that we can continue to express those qualities that have made human civilization. We will survive as animals, but not as human beings that have created civilization out of the splendor of the earth.

—René Dubos, from "The Environmental Apocalypse," in *Eye on the World*, Walter Cronkite, ed.

. . . . .

ESCHATOLOGY

The branch of theology that studies the general area of last things, from the Greek eschatos, *"furthest"; these include many issues touched on here—apocalypses, resurrection, judgment, afterlife, and so forth.*

In every moment slumbers the possibility of being the eschatological moment; you must awaken it.

—Rudolph Bultman, from *Jesus and the Word*

One God, one Law, one element,
And one far-off divine event,
To which the whole creation moves.

—Alfred Tennyson, from *In Memoriam*

It is remarkable to note the extraordinary reticence of the Bible and the Mishna on the subjects of death, resurrection, immortality, the Hereafter, the Judgment Day in the afterlife, Heaven and Hell, and the Messiah—subjects which occupied so large a place in the religions of the Near East, the Greco-Roman world, and Christianity. . . . Eschatology never displaced the original prophetic element in Judaism's vision.

—Abba Hillel Silver, from *Where Judaism Differs*

That was always the charm and the danger of eschatology: destruction must be seen as a positive act, increasing the fund of existence; but what if it should prove a reversion to nonexistence?

—Perry Miller, from *Errand into the Wilderness*

. . . . .

ETERNAL RETURN

In contrast to the linear sense of time, a sine qua non of Western apocalypticism, native American, Asian, and other religious communities have a sense of time as a circularity, universal destruction followed by universal renewal. That which is renewed, though purified (much like in the flood stories), is not a new heaven and a new earth, drastically different, but our good old terrestrial condition, for better and for worse.

Sirs, after the lapse of a hundred thousand years, the cycle is to be renewed; this world will be destroyed; also the mighty ocean will dry up; and this broad earth, and Sumeru, the monarch of the mountain, will be burnt up and destroyed—up to the Brahma world will the destruction of the world extend. Therefore, sirs, cultivate friendliness; cultivate compassion, joy, and indifference; wait on your mothers; wait on your fathers; and honor your elders among your kinfolk.

—from *Buddhism in Translation*
by Henry Clarke Warren

. . . . .

ETERNITY

Eternity's a terrible thought. I mean, where's it going to end?

—Tom Stoppard, from *Rosencrantz and Guildenstern
Are Dead*

Death is not an event in life: we do not live to experience death. If we take eternity to mean not infinite temporal duration but timelessness, then eternal life belongs to those who live in the present.

—Ludwig Wittgenstein, from *Tractatus Logico-Philosophicus*

As if you could kill time without injuring eternity.

—Henry David Thoreau, from "Economy," in *Walden*

. . . . .

EVANGELISM

Evangelist, n: A bearer of good tidings, particularly (in a religious sense) such as assure us of our own salvation and the damnation of our neighbors.

—Ambrose Bierce, from *The Devil's Dictionary*

. . . . .

EVIL

We declare that the Word will some time subdue the whole rational creation and change every soul into his own perfection. . . . For the Word and the healing power in him being stronger than every evil. . . . And the end of all things is to destroy evil.

—Origen, from *Against Celsus*

We need more understanding of human nature, because the only real danger that exists is man himself. . . . We know nothing of man, far too little. His psyche should be studied because we are the origin of all coming evil.

—Carl Jung, from a BBC television interview

The most detestable wickedness, the most horrid cruelties, and the greatest miseries, that have afflicted the human race, have had their origin in this thing called revelation.

—Thomas Paine, from *The Age of Reason*

The fact that the grossest forms of evil enter into history as schemes of redemption and that the Christian faith itself introduces new evils, whenever it pretends that the Christian life, individually or collectively, has achieved a final perfection, gives us a clue to the possibilities and the limits of historic achievement.

—Reinhold Niebuhr, from "Fulfillments in History and the Fulfillment of History," in *Faith and History*

. . . . .

EVOLUTION

Believing as I do that man in the distant future will be a far more perfect creature than he now is, it is intolerable that he be doomed to complete annihilation after such a long-continued process. To those who fully admit the immortality of the human soul, the destruction of our world will not appear so dreadful.

—Charles Darwin

Evolution isn't over . . . the apocalypse will be part of that leap of evolution. . . . By the very definition of apocalypse mankind must cease to exist, at least in a material form . . . it will evolve into a species of pure thought . . . into something well beyond our comprehension . . . into a universal consciousness . . . into God.

—from *Naked*, film written and directed by
Mike Leigh

From an evolutionary point of view, man has stopped moving, if he ever did move.

—Pierre Teilhard de Chardin, from *The Phenomenon
of Man*

. . . . .

EXISTENCE

I stick my finger into existence—it smells of nothing. Where am I? Who am I? How came I here? What is this thing called the world? What does this word mean?

—Søren Kierkegaard, from *Repetition*

All that has achieved existence deserves to be destroyed.

—Johann Wolfgang von Goethe

There is no means of *proving* it is preferable to be than not to be.

—E. M. Cioran, from "Strangled Thoughts," in
The New Gods

I know perfectly well that I don't want to do anything; to do something is to create existence and there's quite enough existence as it is.

—Jean-Paul Sartre, from *Nausea*

. . . . .

EXTINCTION

In one sense, extinction is less terrible than death, since extinction can be avoided, while death is inevitable; but in another sense extinction is more terrible—is the more radical nothingness—because extinction ends death just as surely as it ends birth and life. Death is only death; extinction is the death of death.

—Jonathan Schell, from *The Fate of the Earth*

Master of the thunder-cloud, set the lightning free,
And add the thunder-stone to that and fling them on his head,
For death is all the fashion now, till even Death be dead.

—Sophocles, from *King Oedipus*

f

FAMILY

Zeus will destroy this race of mortals
when children are born gray at the temples.
Children will not resemble their fathers,
and there will be no affection between guest and host
and no love between friends or brothers as in the past.
Sons and daughters will be quick to offend their aging parents
and rebuke them and speak to them with rudeness
and cruelty, not knowing about divine retribution;
they will not even repay their parents for their keep —
these law-breakers — and they will sack one another's cities.

—Hesiod, from "The Five Ages,"
Apostolos Athanassakis, trans.

I do not pretend that there is any way of arriving at the millennium. . . . So long as the present family survives, there will be
unrequited love and parents' tyranny and children's ingratitude;
and if something new were substituted for the family, it would

bring new evils, probably worse. Human life cannot be made a matter of unalloyed bliss, and to allow oneself excessive hopes is to court disappointment.

—Bertrand Russell, from *The Impact of Science on Society*

Brother with brother shall grapple in battle,
Kin that are closest, shall couple and care not,
Harsh shall the world wax, and heedless of whoredoms—
An axe-age, a sword-age, when shields shall be shattered,
A storm-age, a wolf-age, ere the world's ending.

—from *The Edda*

. . . . .

FAMINE

I had a dream, which was not all a dream
All earth was but one thought—and that was death,
Immediate and inglorious; and the pang
Of famine fed upon all entrails—men
Died, and their bones were tombless as their flesh;
The meagre by the meagre were devoured.

—Lord Byron, from "Darkness"

And the land that you now see ruling shall be a trackless waste, and people shall see it desolate.

—2 Esdras 5:3

· · · · ·

FASHIONS

Women sometimes have the problem of trying to judge by artificial light how a dress will look by daylight. That is very like the problem of all of us: to dress our souls not for the electric lights of the present world but for the daylight of the next. The good dress is the one that will face that light. For that light will last longer.

—C. S. Lewis, from *The World's Last Night*

· · · · ·

FIFTIES

In the spring of 1950 I was twenty-four. . . . I was ready to settle down, somewhere near but not in New York City, since the Russians were coming and the Bomb would soon fall in the night.

—Gore Vidal, from "How I Survived the Fifties,"
in *The New Yorker*, Oct. 2, 1995

· · · · ·

FIN DE SIÈCLE

We may not hurry into white gowns or gather on hilltops, but at each century's end, the X's on the calendar do seem darker, do seem to be leading us beyond the run-of-the-mill toward apocalypse.

—Hillel Schwartz in *Century's End*

Nowadays all the married men live like bachelors, and all the bachelors live like married men, said Lady Narborough.

Fin du siècle, murmured Lord Henry.

Fin du globe, answered his hostess.

I wish it were *fin du globe,* said Dorian, with a sigh. Life is a great disappointment.

—Oscar Wilde, from *The Picture of Dorian Gray*

It's a big thing when a century ends, a time of fate and fore-shadowing. . . . The 1890s were a pleasant time, a beautiful epoque, and a prelude to the most killing century in the history of man. Start out on a bicycle built for two, wind up at Verdun.

—Peggy Noonan, from *Life, Liberty and the Pursuit of Happiness*

. . . . .

FIRE

The world, an entity out of everything, was created by neither gods nor men, but was, is, and will be eternally living fire, regularly becoming ignited and regularly becoming extinguished.

—Heraclitus, from *Cosmic Fragments*

The scorched clouds smoke. The mountains
Of earth catch fire, the prairies crack, the rivers
Dry up, the meadows are white-hot, the trees,
The leaves, burn to a crisp, the crops are tinder.
I grieve at minor losses. The great cities
Perish, and their great walls; and nations perish

With all their people: everything is ashes.
The woods and mountains burn . . .
And Mount Olympus . . . the Alps, and the
Cloud-topped Apennines are burning.

And Phaeton sees the earth on fire . . .
Under his feet he feels the chariot glowing . . .
. . . They have their way, the horses.

And that was when, or so men think, the people
Of Africa turned black.

> —Ovid, from *Metamorphoses*, Rolfe Humphries, trans.

And then cometh the season and the end; and my vineyard
will I cause to be burned with fire.

> —*Book of Mormon*, Jacob 5:77

. . . . .

FIRE AND WATER: THE DYNAMIC DUO

Whether in pre-biblical mythologies about the End or in contemporary scenarios of thermonuclear war and melting of the ice cap, these two basic elements, in countless guises and as metaphors for unknown powers within the human heart, are never far away from the scene of the crime—the most popular and efficient smoking guns that do in the universe.

By the word of God heavens existed long ago and an earth was formed out of water and by means of water, through which the world of that time was deluged with water and perished. But by the same word the present heavens and earth have been reserved for fire, being kept until the day of judgment and destruction of the godless.

—2 Peter, 3:5–7

Some say the world will end in fire,
Some say in ice.
From what I've tasted of desire
I hold with those who favor fire.
But if it had to perish twice,
I think I know enough of hate
To say that for destruction ice
Is also great
And would suffice.

—Robert Frost, "Fire and Ice"

It isn't necessary to imagine the world ending in fire and ice. There are two other possibilities: one is paperwork, and the other nostalgia.

—Frank Zappa, from *The Real Frank Zappa Book*

. . . . .

FLOOD

I have determined to make an end of all flesh, for the earth is filled with violence. . . . I am going to bring a flood of waters on the earth, to destroy from under heaven all flesh in which is the breath of life. . . . But I will establish my covenant with you; and you shall come into the ark.

—Genesis, 6:13, 17, 18

Tear down this house, build a ship!
Give up possessions, seek thou life.
Despise property and keep the soul alive!
Aboard the ship take thou the seed of all living things.

—from *The Epic of Gilgamesh*

It is worth remembering for future reference . . . that if the Antarctic ice cap did melt, its melt-water would add nearly 300 feet to the world's sea level—the height of a 30-story building.

—Isaac Asimov and Frederik Pohl, from
Our Angry Earth

The Great Flood was sent because of the large numbers of dirty people.

—from *The Pocket Book of Boners: An Omnibus of
School Boy Howlers and Unconscious Humor*

The only thing that stops God from sending another flood is that the first one was useless.

—Nicolas Chamfort

Society is heading for the Big Flush, and we're going to be the ones clinging to the rim while everything else goes down.

—from *Survivors*, film written by Michael Leesan,
directed by Michael Ritchie

. . . . .

FOUR HORSEMEN OF THE APOCALYPSE

I looked, and there was a white horse! Its rider had a bow . . . and he came out conquering and to conquer. When he opened the second seal . . . out came another horse, bright red; its rider was permitted to take peace from the earth, so that people would slaughter one another. . . . I looked, and there was a black horse! Its rider held a pair of scales in his hand. . . . When he opened the fourth seal . . . I looked and there was a pale green horse! Its rider's name was Death.

—Revelation 6:1–8

. . . . .

FUND-RAISING

The human race is a pilot project that's failed: Denied future funding!

—Belinda Plutz

. . . . .

FUTURE

When I look into the future, it's so bright it burns my eyes.

—Oprah Winfrey

The trouble with our times is that the future is not what it used to be.

—Paul Valéry

The planet's survival has become so uncertain that any effort, any thought that presupposes an assured future amounts to a mad gamble.

—Elias Canetti, from *The Secret Heart of the Clock: Notes, Aphorisms, Fragments, 1973–1985*

It may be in the larger design of the universe this invasion from Mars is not without its ultimate benefit for men; it has robbed us of that serene confidence in the future which is the most fruitful source of decadence.

—H. G. Wells, from *The War of the Worlds*

I never think of the future. It comes soon enough.

—Albert Einstein

What will America do—what *can* America do—with an implacable prophecy that there is a point in time beyond which the very concept of a future becomes meaningless? Protestant America, as well as Catholic, has an implicit commitment to this event.

—Perry Miller, from *Errand into the Wilderness*

Nation will rise against nation, and kingdom against kingdom: there will be great earthquakes, and in various places famines and plagues; and there will be dreadful portents and great signs from heaven.

—Luke 21:10–11

If you can look into the seeds of time,
And say which grain will grow and which will not,
Speak then to me.

—William Shakespeare, from *Macbeth*

G

GERMS

Watching television, you'd think we lived at bay, in total jeopardy, surrounded on all sides by human-seeking germs, shielded against infection and death only by a chemical technology that enables us to keep killing them off.

—Lewis Thomas, from "Germs," in *The Lives of a Cell*

Filmmakers will undoubtedly learn to use fear of disease the way they once used the threat of nuclear catastrophe, which enhanced ordinary race-against-the-clock suspense with the possibility of apocalypse. Something was bound to succeed the bomb as the ultimate terror generator in big-budget thrillers, and virus is the strongest, most charismatic candidate to come along in years.

—Terence Rafferty, from "The Enemy Within,"
in *The New Yorker*, March 20, 1995

In 1933 we thought an apocalypse of germ warfare was coming to wipe out civilization.

—Freeman Dyson, recollections, on PBS,
New York, June 16, 1994

In the nineteenth century men lost their fear of God and acquired a fear of microbes.

—Anonymous

. . . . .

GLOBAL COOLING

They knew not what dim hours went on, went by,
For while they slept the clock stopt newly wound
As the cold hardened . . .
The coldness seemed more night, the coldness deepened
As a sound deepens into silences . . .
The earth was cooling and drew down the sky.
The air was crumbling. There was no more sky.

—Gordon Bottomley, from "The End of the World"

. . . . .

GLOBAL WARMING

It is not commonly realized how near the death temperature a large fraction of the human species lives . . . the margin of safety of much of the Earth amounts to no more than 20 degrees. . . . Thousands of millions between the latitudes of Cairo and the Cape of Good Hope were subjected to a choking atmosphere that grew damper and hotter inexorably from day to day. All human movement ceased. There was nothing to be done but to lie panting, as a dog pants in hot weather.

—Fred Hoyle, from *The Black Cloud*

. . . . .

Gog

Gog and Magog, the frightening and mysterious allies of Satan, are scheduled to make their appearance in the final struggle against the returning Jesus at the end of the Millennium.

On that day, when Gog comes against the land of Israel . . . the fish of the sea, and the birds of the air, and the animals of the field . . . and all human beings that are on the face of the earth, shall quake at my presence, and the mountains shall be thrown down, and the cliffs shall fall, and every wall shall tumble to the ground.

—Ezekiel 38:18–20

Ezekiel tells us that Gog, the nation that will lead all of the other powers of darkness against Israel, will come out of the north. Biblical scholars have been saying for generations that Gog must be Russia. What other powerful nation is to the north of Israel? None. But it didn't seem to make sense before the Russian revolution, when Russia was a Christian country. Now it does, now that Russia has become communistic and atheistic, now that Russia has set itself against God. Now it fits the description of Gog perfectly.

—Ronald Reagan, in a 1971 address to California
legislators

When the thousand years are ended, Satan will be released from his prison and will come out to deceive the nations at the four corners of the earth, Gog and Magog, in order to gather them for battle; they are as numerous as the sands of the sea.

—Revelation 20:7–8

. . . . .

GOOD SAMARITANS

When there was an accident [on the road] and someone was hurt, a man stopped. . . . But today a man saves his family and to hell with everyone else. Already millions must be dead. . . . And the war was less than a half hour old. So one stranger on the roadside meant nothing. . . . With the use of the hydrogen bomb, the Christian era was dead, and with it must die the tradition of the Good Samaritan.

—Pat Frank, from *Alas, Babylon*

H

HANGING

There are times when one would like to hang the whole human race and finish the farce.

—Mark Twain, from *A Connecticut Yankee in King Arthur's Court*

. . . . .

HAPPINESS

The wine dries up, the vine languishes, all the merry-hearted sigh. The mirth of the timbrels is stilled, the noise of the jubilant has ceased, the mirth of the lyre is stilled.

—Isaiah 24:7–8

MRS. KNOX: It's like in the book of Revelation. But I do say that when people have happiness within themselves, all the earthquakes, all the floods, and all the prisons in the world can't make them really unhappy.

—George Bernard Shaw, from *Fanny's First Play*

. . . . .

HEAVEN

The glory of the next world will never wear out.

—John Bunyan, from *The Pilgrim's Progress*

And the street of the city is pure gold, transparent as glass.

—Revelation 21:21

On the palm-trees in Heaven each cluster yields ten thousand dates, and on the fig-trees each shoot yields ten thousand figs, and if three men were to partake of one fig all of them would be satisfied.

—from the *Apocalypse of James the Brother of Jesus*

Heaven—the Coney Island of the Christian imagination

—Elbert Hubbard, from *Roycroft Dictionary and Book of Epigrams*

When I watched all the children, their copper, brown, and beige faces staring up at me as I taught Sunday school, I felt that I was committing a crime in talking about the gentle Jesus, in telling them to reconcile themselves to their misery on earth in order to gain the crown of eternal life. Were only Negroes to gain this crown? Was Heaven, then, merely to be another ghetto?

—James Baldwin, from *The Fire Next Time*

Heaven, as conventionally conceived, is a place so inane, so dull, so useless, so miserable, that nobody has ever ventured to describe a whole day in heaven, though plenty of people have described a day at the seaside.

—George Bernard Shaw, from *Misalliance*

Each people has as much heaven over its head as it has land under its feet.

—Chaim Nachman Bialik

In the world to come there is no eating or drinking or procreation or trading or jealousy or hatred or competition, but the righteous sit with crowns on their heads feasting on the radiance of the Shechina.

—from the *Mishna, Berachot*

The trouble with kingdoms of heaven on earth is that they're liable to come to pass, and then their fraudulence is apparent for all to see. We need a Kingdom of Heaven in Heaven, if only because it can't be "realized."

—Malcolm Muggeridge, from "Me and Myself" in
Jesus Rediscovered

. . . . .

HELL

Humans don't know this but due to the war among the angels, heaven's closed. Nobody who has died since the beginning of time has made it in. Sorry. All those bones just lying there! But, Hell! While heaven may be closed, I [Lucifer] am open all year round, even on Christmas.

—from *The Prophecy*, film written and
directed by Gregory Widen

Abandon all hope, ye who enter here.

—Dante Alighieri, inscription at Hell's entrance,
from "Inferno," in *The Divine Comedy*

Sheol [Hell] beneath is stirred up to meet you when you come. . . . Maggots are the bed beneath you, and worms are your covering.

—Isaiah 14:9, 11

Hell is a city much like London.

—Percy Bysshe Shelley, from *Peter Bell the Third*

So this is hell. I'd never have believed it. You remember all we were told about the torture chambers, the fire and brimstone, the "burning marl." Old wives' tales! There's no need for red-hot pokers. Hell is other people.

—Jean-Paul Sartre, from *No Exit*

Hell is oneself;
Hell is alone, the other figures in it
Merely projections. There is nothing
to escape from
And nothing to escape to. One is always alone.

—T. S. Eliot, from *The Cocktail Party*

Hell is paved with the skulls of priests.

—St. John Chrysostom, from *De sacerdotie*

Hell is paved with good intentions.

—John Ray, from *English Proverbs*

. . . . .

HIROSHIMA

Rest in Peace. The mistake shall not be repeated.

—cenotaph at Hiroshima

We knew we were standing
Where the end of the world began.

—L. Williams Hubbel, from "At Hiroshima," in
Seventy Poems

. . . . .

HISTORY

What until recently seemed to be only the apocalyptic fantasies of the Christian faith has today entered the sphere of the soberest scientific calculus; the sudden end of history.

—Emil Brunner, from *Eternal Hope*

The fading away of the cold war has brought an era of ideological conflict to an end. But it has not, as forecast, brought an end to history.

—Arthur M. Schlesinger, Jr., from
The Disuniting of America

. . . . .

HOLOCAUST

The right vantage point from which to view a holocaust is that of a corpse, but from that vantage point, of course, there is nothing to report.

—Jonathan Schell, from *The Fate of the Earth*

What for Hitler . . . was among the war's main objectives . . . and what for Eichmann was a job . . . was for the Jews quite literally the end of the world.

—Hannah Arendt, from *Eichmann in Jerusalem*

What we realize when we have read the precious book [of Revelation] a few times is that John the Divine had on the face of it a grandiose scheme for wiping out and annihilating everybody who wasn't of the elect, the chosen people, in short, and of climbing up himself right on to the throne of God.

— D. H. Lawrence, from *Apocalypse*

. . . . .

HOPE

In our sad condition, our only consolation is the expectancy of another life.

— Martin Luther

The experience of four thousand years should enlarge our hopes, and diminish our apprehensions. . . . No people, unless the face of nature is changed, will relapse into their original barbarism.

— Edward Gibbon, from *Decline and Fall of the Roman Empire*

I

IMAGINATION

Is it a failure of my imagination
that I cannot believe in the end of the world
or that I believe in it, quietly, as I do in death
but in its own good time.

> —Harvey Shapiro, from "Last Things,"
> in *National Cold Storage Company*

The imagination is always at the end of an era.

> —Wallace Stevens

. . . . .

IMMORTALITY

Millions long for immortality who do not know what to do
with themselves on a rainy Sunday afternoon.

> —Susan Ertz, from *Anger in the Sky*

I don't want to achieve immortality through my work . . . I want to achieve it through not dying.

—Woody Allen

To himself everyone is an immortal. He may know that he is going to die, but he can never know that he is dead.

—Samuel Butler, from his notebooks

He had decided to live forever or die in the attempt.

—Joseph Heller, from *Catch-22*

Deathlessness should be arrived at in a . . . haphazard fashion. Loving fame as much as any man, we shall carve our initials in the shell of a tortoise and turn him loose in a peat bog.

—E. B. White, from "Immortality," in *The New Yorker*, March 28, 1936

. . . . .

INCONSEQUENCE

Man a little eccentric species of animal, which—fortunately—has its day; all on earth a mere moment, an accident, an exception without consequences, something of no importance to the general character of the earth; the earth itself, like every star, a hiatus between two nothingnesses.

—Friedrich Nietzsche, from *The Will to Power*

A man said to the universe,
"Sir, I exist!"
"However," replied the universe,
"The fact has not created in me
A sense of obligation."

—Stephen Crane, from "War Is Kind"

. . . . .

INEVITABILITY

Everything indeed, everything visible in nature or established in theory, suggests that the universe is implacably progressing toward final darkness and decay.

—Lincoln Barnett, from *The Universe and Dr. Einstein*

It is all
A moment. The trees
Grow earthward: neither good
Nor evil, hopes nor fears.
Repulsion nor desire,
Earth, water, air or fire
Will serve to stay the fall.

—Robert Lowell, from "Lord Weary's Castle"

. . . . .

INFORMATION

Just as a Christian might contend that the body is merely a temporary encasement for the everlasting spirit that resides in it, the new cosmologists would contend that the body is merely a temporary encasement for the information that gives rise to it. . . . For our heirs, the path to eternal life will be paved with ream upon ream of informational readouts.

—Jeremy Rifkin, from *Algeny*

. . . . .

INTERNET

Is the end of the world near? . . . The road to *our* Armageddon is similar to Lot's in Sodom, says Jesus. . . . We want sex, hard and brutal, on our TV sets more and more. . . . We are guilty of sinful pleasure and idolatry. . . . One of the last directions a nation takes before the end is perverted sex . . . hate, kiddie porn, bestiality, it's all there on the Internet.

—Billy Graham, from his sermon, "Is the End of the World Near?" delivered in Toronto, Sept. 9, 1995

. . . . .

ISLAM

When the sun shall be darkened,
When the stars shall be thrown down,

When the pregnant camels shall be neglected,
When the savage beasts shall be mustered,
When the seas shall be set boiling,
When the souls shall be coupled,
When the buried infant shall be asked for
    what sin she was slain,
When the scrolls shall be unrolled,
When the heaven shall be stripped off,
When Hell shall be set blazing,
When Paradise shall be brought nigh,
Then shall a soul know what it has produced.

—"The Darkening" from the Koran 81:1–14

. . . . .

ISLAM, NATION OF

According to Elijah (Muhammad) the "so-called American Negro" is the only reason Allah has permitted the United States to endure so long; the white man's time was up in 1913, but it is the will of Allah that this lost black nation, the black men of this country, be redeemed from their white masters and returned to the true faith, which is Islam. Until this is done—and it will be accomplished very soon—the total destruction of the white man is being delayed.

—James Baldwin, from *The Fire Next Time*

J

JEHOVAH'S WITNESSES

Founded in 1884 by Charles Taze Russell, the Jehovah's Witnesses, officially the Watchtower Bible and Tract Society, is among the most eschatological of Christian denominations. They have predicted the beginning of the end for 1914 (the start of World War One), for 1948 (at the time of the ingathering of the Jews into the new State of Israel), and for numerous other dates.

Do we see a parallel between the turmoil during the twilight years of Judah under her kings and the turmoil in Christendom today? Certainly we do! Today, as in Jeremiah's day, the approach to the end of a system of things is marked by the shedding of oceans of innocent blood, notably in the two world wars of this century.

—from *The Watchtower*, March 1, 1994

. . . . .

JERUSALEM

In that day the mountains shall drip sweet wine, the hills shall
flow with milk . . . Egypt shall become a desolation. . . . But
Judah shall be inhabited forever, and Jerusalem to all generations.

—Joel 3:18–20

Then I saw a new heaven and a new earth; for the first heaven
and the first earth had passed away, and sea was no more. And I
saw the holy city, the new Jerusalem, coming down out of
heaven from God, prepared as a bride adorned for her husband.

—Revelation 21:1–2

So part we sadly in this troublous world,
To meet with joy in sweet Jerusalem.

—William Shakespeare, from *Henry VI, Part 3*

I will not cease from Mental Fight,
Nor shall my Sword sleep in my hand
Till we have built Jerusalem
In England's green and pleasant Land.

—William Blake, from *Milton*

Raoul closed his big brown eyes to picture Jerusalem. He saw
rocks and robes and gold domes and donkeys. He didn't see any
angels, but he knew they were hanging around. Jerusalem was

where it all went down, man. It was connected to heaven like Spanish Harlem was connected to Puerto Rico.

—Tom Robbins, from *Skinny Legs and All*

. . . . .

JEWS

The Jew is the emblem of eternity. He whom neither slaughter nor torture of thousands of years could destroy. . . . He who was the first to produce the oracles of God . . . the guardian of prophecy. . . . The Jew is everlasting as eternity itself.

—Leo Tolstoy

For some time I believed that the Jews' [return to Israel] were a sign [of the apocalypse], a clue to the mystery, a telltale bent twig, a blazed sapling in an otherwise riotous senseless jungle.

But now it appears the Jews may have not left North Carolina after all, and in fact are making porno flicks and building condos and villas in Highlands, enjoying the leaves, and in general behaving like everyone else. There goes the last sign.

—Walker Percy, from *The Second Coming*

The art of the Jews is in the sense of doom.

—Kahlil Gibran, from "The Arts of the Nations," in *Spiritual Sayings*

. . . . .

JEWS, CONVERSION OF

In much apocalyptic literature, the conversion of the Jews is a necessary sign and a precondition for the return of Jesus and the inauguration of the world's end. The requirements, based on Daniel, Revelation, and other apocalyptic texts are 1) physical ingathering to Israel, 2) rebuilding of the Temple, and 3) conversion as the final battles kick in and it becomes clear to all who can see that the Jews were wrong originally and Jesus is truly the Messiah. Such theological requirements account, in part, for Christianity's long torment of the Jews but also for its reluctance (perhaps until the Holocaust) to try to wipe them out completely—who would be left to convert? The positive side of Christian fixation on the people from whom they have sprung has been, of course, the long tradition of Christian Hebraicism. A significant facet of the Puritans' world view and Oliver Cromwell's decision to readmit the Jews to England, after an exile of 400 years, can be seen in this light.

> Had we but world enough, and time,
> This coyness, lady, were no crime . . .
> . . . I would love you ten years before the flood:
> And you should, if you please, refuse
> Till the conversion of the Jews.
>
> —Andrew Marvell, from "To His Coy Mistress"

It is extremely difficult for a Jew to be converted, for how can he bring himself to believe in the divinity of—another Jew?

—Heinrich Heine (attributed)

The Nation of Israel is God's prophetic time clock.

—Pat Robertson, from *The Secret Kingdom*

It is a familiar theme in the conversation and heart of the faithful, that in the last days before the judgment the Jews shall believe in the true Christ, that is, our Christ.

—St. Augustine, from *City of God*

Of the three prerequisites to bring about the end of days, [Chuck] Buck [an American evangelist] explained, two already have been fulfilled. Israel is already in the hands of the Jews, and Jerusalem is a Jewish city. All that remains to be accomplished now is to rebuild the Temple, which will, sorry to say, have to be destroyed again for the third and last time in order to precipitate, first, the great Rapture, in which all eyes will see who is damned and who is saved, and then, the war to end all wars, the show-down at Megiddo, Armageddon, the battle of Gog and Magog— Apocalypse.

—Tova Reich, from *The Jewish War*

L

LANGUAGE

"The end of the world?" Here thinking makes a sharp turn and whistles in the dark. And it does so convincingly, because the End of the World is surely in today's language an expression of merriment: witness how it is used so often as a jolly foil—"It is not the end of the world." And if it were? If the end came it would be unrecognizable; nothing rooted in being can define not being.

—Rudolf Baranik, artist statement

The question seriously arises whether the court, in Los Angeles, becomes the creature of Johnnie Cochran, whose use of apocalyptic rhetoric transforms the question, "Did he do it or did he not do it?" to the question, "Do you believe in God or do you not believe in God . . . ?"

—William F. Buckley, Jr., in the *New York Post*, Oct. 2, 1995

. . . . .

Last Judgment

There's no need to stand about waiting for the Last Judgment—it takes place every day.

—Albert Camus, from *The Fall*

And these are some of the survivors of that Judgment. Such nice people! And the civilization they represent—that's nice too. No heights or abysses, but plenty of milk for the kids, and a reasonably high average IQ, and everything, in a quiet provincial way, thoroughly cozy and sensible and human.

—Aldous Huxley, from *Ape and Essence*

GOD: We've had a lot of administrative problems here, so for convenience's sake, we've decided to send last names beginning A through M to Heaven, and last names N through Z we'll be sending to Hell. Maiden names only, ladies, I take you the way you were born.

—Mark O'Donnell, from *That's It, Folks*

. . . . .

Last Night

What if this present were the world's last night?
Mark in my heart, O Soul, where thou dost dwell,

The picture of Christ crucified, and tell
Whether that countenance can thee affright.

> —John Donne, from "What if this present were the
> world's last night?"

The doctrine of the Second Coming has failed, so far as we are concerned, if it does not make us realize that at every moment of every year in our lives Donne's question "What if this present were the world's last night?" is equally relevant.

> —C. S. Lewis, from *The World's Last Night*

. . . . .

LAW ENFORCEMENT

It is not uncommon for dedicated, militant believers in global destruction and salvation to find themselves in dangerous confrontations with police or military forces. The nature of militant millennialism almost demands it, for it is an axiom of the millennium that this world is so far from human redemption that only God's action can rescue it from Satan's control.

> —Ted Daniels, from *Millennial Prophecy Report*

. . . . .

LOS ANGELES

Perhaps there is no life after death . . . there's just Los Angeles.

> —Rich Anderson, in *1,911 Best Things Anybody
> Ever Said*, Robert T. Byrne, ed.

Surveying the [earthquake] damage in Los Angeles, Bill Clinton confessed to being amazed by the collapsed freeways and miles of damaged buildings. Like many forgetful natives and startled visitors, he discovered the fearfulness California can display—a combination of the sublime and the apocalyptic sufficient to sharpen anyone's sense of an ending. . . . L.A. writers have specialized in depicting Final Days.

—David Reid, from "Where Apocalypse Is Never Far
Away," in the *New York Times*, Jan. 26, 1994

. . . . .

LOVE

Then what will love be in the future, she wondered, lying on him cheek pressed against his, a dancing with him in the Carolina moonlight with the old world and time before you, or a cleaving to him at the world's end, and which is better?

—Walker Percy, from *The Second Coming*

Love is the final end of the world's history, the Amen of the Universe.

—Novalis, from *Hymns and Thoughts on Religion*

M

MAD

The Lord will roar from on high . . . against all the inhabitants of the earth. The clamor will resound to the ends of the earth.

—Jeremiah 25:30–31

The bow of God's wrath is bent, and the arrow made ready on the string, and justice bends the arrow at your heart, and strains the bow, and there is nothing but the mere pleasure of God, and that of an angry God, without any promise or obligation at all, that keeps the arrow one moment from being made drunk with your blood.

—Jonathan Edwards, from *Sinners in the Hands of an Angry God*

．．．．．

MAIL ORDER

When the End comes there will be no supermarkets and there will be no drugstores, but there will always be mail order.

—from *Survivors*, film written by Michael Leesan,
directed by Michael Ritchie

．．．．．

MARTIANS

Their [Martian] world is far gone in its cooling and this world is still crowded with life, but crowded only with what they regard as inferior animals. To carry warfare sunward is, indeed, their only escape from the destruction that generation after generation creeps upon them.

. . . Way! Way! The Martians are coming!

—H. G. Wells, from *The War of the Worlds*

First we need enough Minutemen to be sure that we destroy all those Russian cities. Then we need Polaris missiles to follow in order to tear up the foundations to a depth of ten feet. . . . Then, when all Russia is silent, and when no air defenses are left, we want waves of aircraft to drop enough bombs to tear the whole place up and down to a depth of forty feet to prevent the Martians recolonizing the country. And to hell with the fallout.

—U.S. Assistant Secretary of Defense to Sir Solly
Zuckerman, chief scientific advisor to British Ministry
of Defense, quoted in *War* by Gwynne Dyer

. . . . .

MASS DESTRUCTION

Howls the Whirlwind Over the World
Tempests Quaking Shake the World
The Earthquake Opens Abrupt the World,
Cold Dreadful Mass Destruction.

—Richard Eberhart, from "World War"

A World is sooner destroyed than made.

—Thomas Burnet, from *The Sacred Theory
of the Earth*

. . . . .

MAYA

It turns out that the Maya, the most scientifically advanced people in the area of present-day Belize, Guatemala, and Mexico, simply walked away from their civilization nearly 1,000 years ago. . . . Incidentally, they predicted that the world would end on Sunday, Dec. 23, 2012. Jot it down.

—John J. O'Conner from "Ultimate Rerun: History,"
in the *New York Times*, July 1995

Finally on the last page of the manuscript [the Dresden Codex of Mayan hieroglyphics] is depicted the Destruction of the World. . . . Great streams of water gush from the sun and moon. The old goddess, she of the tiger claws and forbidding as-

pect, the malevolent patroness of floods and cloudbursts, over-
turns the bowl of the heavenly waters. . . . Below with downward
pointed spear, symbolic of the universal destruction, the black
God stalks abroad, a screeching owl raging on his fearsome head.
Here, indeed, is portrayed with graphic touch the final all-
engulfing cataclysm.

> —from "An Introduction to the Study of the Maya
> Hieroglyphics," a bulletin of the Bureau of American
> Ethnology by Sylvanus G. Morley

. . . . .

MEANINGLESSNESS

Tomorrow, and tomorrow, and tomorrow,
Creeps in this petty pace from day to day,
To the last syllable of recorded time;
. . . It is a tale
Told by an idiot, full of sound and fury,
Signifying nothing.

> —William Shakespeare, from *Macbeth*

If after all that we have lived and thought,
All comes to Nought,—
If there be nothing after Now,
And we be nothing anyhow,
And we know that,—why live?

> —Edwin Arlington Robinson, from "The Man
> Against the Sky"

. . . . .

MEDIA

"The whole world is about to explode . . . what do you do?"
"I wonder where to put the camera."

—from *Groundhog Day*, film written by
Harold Ramis and Danny Rubin,
directed by Harold Ramis

If some great catastrophe is not announced every morning, we feel a certain void: "Nothing in the paper today," we sigh.

—Paul Valéry

List of Important Religion Stories for August: 1. Conflict over abortion and violence. 2. Episcopal Church's proposed sexuality guidelines. 3. Vatican stance toward the Cairo population conference. 4. Vacation Bible camps. 5. Imminent destruction of the world by fire and Last Judgment (only if time permits).

—Peter Steinfels, from the *New York
Times*, Aug. 20, 1994

. . . . .

MEDITATION

What is the significance of meditative practices in the modern world, particularly as the "extinction" clock reads two minutes to midnight? . . . Is enlightenment more important than saving the world? Or is enlightenment the only way of saving the world? . . . It is time for inner city meditators. . . . Time for spiritual warriors to taste the toxic garbage of a collapsing ecology. If there is to be any more "time."

—Rudolph Wurlitzer, in *Hard Travel to Sacred Places*

. . . . .

MEMORY

What has kept the world safe from the bomb since 1945 has not been deterrence, in the sense of fear of specific weapons, so much as it's been memory. The memory of what happened at Hiroshima.

—John Hersey, interviewed in *Writers at Work*,
George Plimpton, ed.

. . . . .

MESSIAH

Then they will see the Son of Man coming in a cloud . . . and great glory. Now when these things begin to take place, stand up and raise your heads, because your redemption is drawing near.

—Luke 21:27

The Messiah will come only when he is no longer necessary; he will come only on the day after his arrival.

—Franz Kafka, from *Parables*

Where is the Messiah when we need her?

—bumper sticker sighted in New Haven, Connecticut

An architect of hidden worlds, every pious Jew is, partly, the Messiah.

—Abraham Joshua Heschel, from *The Earth Is the Lord's*

David's son comes only in an age which is either completely guilty or completely innocent.

—*Talmud, Baba Bathra*

I believe with perfect faith in the coming of the Messiah. And even if he is late in coming, nevertheless I believe.

—Moses Maimonides

I would be happy to care for the baby Messiah until its parents are on their feet and have their own place.

—Diane Ravitch, in the *New York Times*, Jan. 7, 1996

. . . . .

MESSIAHS, FALSE

And if anyone says to you at that time, "Look! Here is the Messiah!" or "Look! There he is!"—do not believe it. False messiahs and false prophets will appear and produce signs and omens, to lead astray, if possible, the elect. But be alert; I have already told you everything.

—Mark 13:21–23

He *is* the Messiah [referring to Grand Rabbi Menachem Mendel Schneerson of the Lubavitcher Hasidim, Brooklyn, New York].

—Rabbi Shmuel Butman, in the *New York Times*,
June 14, 1994

The world will end sometime within the next few years, say Ruth Riddle, Wayne Thiebedeau, and Catherine Matteson [survivors of the Waco attack], and they are waiting for David Koresh to return.

—Diane Sawyer, on *Turning Point*, Aug. 3, 1994

Those who believe the Messiah has a super-human nature are guilty of idolatry.

—M. Friedlander, from *Jewish Religion*

. . . . .

METAPHOR

A world ends when its metaphor has died.

—Archibald MacLeish, from "Hypocrite Auteur"

. . . . .

MICKEY MOUSE

[Michael] Eisner knew the world was ending, and he was a fun-oriented guy. Ending with all the C.E.O.s flying their private jets into each other was not a fun way to go. Keeping people at work, however, meant millions could still afford mouse ears. A world ending in mouse ears is not only fun. It's good business.

—Russell Baker, from "Waves of the Future," the *New York Times*, Sept. 9, 1995

. . . . .

MILLENNIUM

Because this period of a thousand years is the unit of duration by which so much of Western history has been chronicled, it is profoundly freighted with symbolism, the sense of change, and perhaps dread. As a technical Christian apocalyptic term, it is the period announced by miraculous happenings (raptures) and great suffering (tribulations) understood to be the work of Antichrist, Satan's human helper. At the end of the millennium, Satan himself breaks away from his thousand-year prison term and, entirely unrehabilitated, is loosed upon the world for one last fling at us. This time, however, the Devil is firmly downed by the returned Jesus, thus ushering in judgment, obliteration, and, finally, new heaven and new earth.

This concept is particularly important to the interpretations of contemporary American fundamentalists who theorize about the End. If you believe Jesus' arrival—the Second Coming—precedes, that is, ushers in the millennium, you are a premillennialist. If you believe Jesus returns only far in the future, after a thousand years of peace and Christianization, you're a postmillennialist. If you believe the present age is the millennium here already, spiritualized (at least potentially) within each human heart, you are an amillennialist.

A millennium is something like a centennial, only it has more legs.

—from *The Pocket Books of Boners: An Omnibus of School Boy Howlers and Unconscious Humor*

But do not ignore this one fact, beloved, that with the Lord one day is like a thousand years, and a thousand years are like one day.

—2 Peter 3:8

Although we have yet to make our peace with a long midcentury of racism and genocide, a new millennium holds out the promise of absolution or, at least, forgiveness or, at the very least, forgetfulness.

—Hillel Schwartz, from *Century's End*

Millennia come and millennia go. Mankind experiences a sort of global grand mal seizure, twitches and froths for a while, shivers the night away in nameless apprehension, clutches at the certitudes offered by false prophets . . . roars and weeps and keens and rends garments—and then, as the great forces of life and belief, from the tides of the ocean to the price-earning ratio of securities, revert back to the mean, as they must, settles down.

—Michael M. Thomas, from "The World Goes Nuts: Kato, Rush—Aaaah!" in the *New York Observer*, May 15, 1995

My own anxiety is not that we will be destroyed by an Antichrist but that despite the countless books, movies and retrospectives about to appear, we will never grasp the meaning of what is about to happen. What is there to say about an event of this size? How do you break its veneer of icy perfection? The very idea of the millennium forces a kind of studied focus on the trivial, an avoidance of our own insignificance.

> —D. T. Max, from "The Millennium Approaches: What to Do?" in the *New York Times*, Oct. 10, 1995

You know how I know it's the end of the world? Everything's been tried . . . every single bubble gum flavor. How we gonna get through the next thousand years?

> —from *Strange Days*, film written by James Cameron and Jay Cocks, directed by Katherine Bigelow

．　．　．　．　．

MILLERITES

The followers of William Miller, a midnineteenth-century New Englander with an unshakable belief in Biblical prophecy, provide a well-documented paradigm of a repeated challenge faced by apocalyptic groups, particularly those with a penchant for specific, dated predictions of the last exit: namely, what happens when the heralded date arrives and the End fails to occur? How does the group of ardent believers manage the disappointing outcome, and what is the aftermath?

Miller's calculations, based largely on Daniel, led him to declare the world would end in 1843 or 1844. When the far-end date passed with no sign of the Second Coming, anti-Millerite editorialists jeered:

"What!—not gone up yet?—We thought you'd gone up! Aren't you going up soon?—Wife didn't go up and leave you behind to burn, did she?"

—Leon Festinger, Henry W. Riecken,
and Stanley Schachter, from *When Prophecy Fails*

Poor William Miller in 1843. Miller (whom I take to have been an honest fanatic) dated the Second Coming to the year, the day, and the very minute. A timely comet fostered the delusion. Thousands waited for the Lord at midnight on March 21st, and went home to a late breakfast on the 22nd followed by the jeers of a drunkard.

—C. S. Lewis, from *The World's Last Night*

. . . . .

MISOGYNY

Everything that has the smell of a woman will be destroyed. Woman is the capsheaf of the abomination of desolation—full of deviltry. In a short time the world will take fire and be dissolved—it is combustible already. All women not obedient had better become so as soon as possible.

—Robert Matthews, alias the Prophet Matthias, from
*Matthias and His Impostures: or, the Progress of
Fanaticism* by William L. Stone

. . . . .

MULTICULTURALISM

It is an ardently advocated, veritably messianic political program, and like most political programs that have succumbed to the utopian temptation, it does not take kindly to true difference.

—Richard Bernstein, from *Dictatorship of Virtue:
Multiculturalism and the Battle for America's Future*

The one absolutely certain way of bringing this nation to ruin, of preventing all possibility of its continuing to be a nation at all would be to permit it to become a tangle of squabbling nationalities, an intricate knot of German-Americans, Irish-Americans, English-Americans, French-Americans, Scandinavian-Americans, or Italian-Americans, each preserving its separate nationality.

—Theodore Roosevelt, from his *Works*

. . . . .

MUSIC

When the music's over
. . . turn out the lights
. . . music is your only friend
until the end
until the end
until the end.

—The Doors, from "When the Music's Over"

So when the last and dreadful Hour
This crumbling Pageant shall devour,
The TRUMPET shall be heard on high.
The dead shall live, the living die,
And MUSICK shall untune the sky.

—John Dryden, from "Song for Saint Cecilia's Day"

People do not want words—they want the sound of battle . . .
the battle of destiny.

—Gamal Abdel Nasser, in a speech to the
National Assembly, 1969

. . . . .

MUTUAL ASSURED DESTRUCTION

We may be likened to two scorpions in a bottle, each capable
of killing the other, but only at the risk of his own life.

—Robert Oppenheimer, quoted in *The New Yorker*,
June 19, 1995

It may be that we shall by a process of sublime irony have
reached a stage in this story where safety will be the sturdy child
of terror, and survival the twin brother of annihilation.

—Winston Churchill, on the hydrogen bomb news
reports of March 3, 1955

. . . . .

MYSTERY

In weighing the fate of the earth and, with it, our own fate, we stand before a mystery, and in tampering with the earth we tamper with a mystery. We are in deep ignorance.

—Jonathan Schell, from *The Fate of the Earth*

N

NAGASAKI

How noble, how splendid was that holocaust of August 9, when flames soared up from the cathedral, dispelling the darkness of war and bringing the light of peace! . . . Eight thousand people together with their priests, burning with pure smoke, entered into eternal life.

—Nagai Takashi, from *The Bells of Nagasaki*

. . . . .

NATIONALISM

No country without an atom bomb could properly consider itself independent.

—Charles de Gaulle, in the *New York Times*,
May 12, 1968

German Christians are being given the awful alternative of consciously wishing for the destruction of their nation so that Christian civilization can survive or wishing for the victory of their nation and thereby the destruction of civilization. I know which alternative I must choose.

—Dietrich Bonhoeffer, in a letter to Reinhold Niebuhr, quoted in the *New York Times*, Feb. 5, 1996

And the wind shifts
and the dust on a doorsill shifts
and even the writing of their footprints
tells us nothing, nothing at all
about the greatest city, the greatest nation
where the strong men listened
and the women warbled; Nothing like us ever was.

—Carl Sandburg, from "Four Preludes on Playthings of the Wind," in *Smoke and Steel*

. . . . .

NATURE

The destructive forces of nature were like a reservoir, dammed up by a thin, unsteady wall, which at any moment might burst, and sweep away the pretentious homunculi who had dared to maintain that man was the measure of all things.

—Kenneth Clark, from *Leonardo da Vinci*

There are no accidents, only nature throwing her weight around. Even the bomb merely releases energy that nature has put there. Nuclear war would be just a spark in the grandeur of space. Nor can radiation "alter" nature; she will absorb it all. After the bomb, nature will pick up the cards we have spilled, shuffle them, and begin her game again.

—Camille Paglia, from *Sexual Personae*

. . . . .

NERO

The brutal Roman emperor and slaughterer of early Christians, whom he blamed for a catastrophic fire that destroyed half of Rome in 64 C.E. Because of his persecutions—among the victims, some believe, was Saint Paul—Nero was a profoundly hated man among the Christians. Even after his death he was feared, as if the allegedly divine power of the Roman emperor were somehow now joined in the popular imagination with tenets of the new religion into a widespread anxiety that Nero would rise from the dead to wreak more havoc. Nero's legend, complete with sightings of the resurrected tyrant, mimicked the power of Jesus, and he thus became an early model for that arch mimic, the Antichrist.

When we asked him about the end of the world, he told us that Nero and the Antichrist were to come first. Nero will rule in the western region after subduing the ten kings. . . . Then Nero himself will be destroyed by the Antichrist so that the whole world and all nations may be drawn under his power until that wicked one is destroyed by the coming of Christ.

—Sulpicius Severus, from *Dialogues*, Bernard McGinn, trans.

. . . . .

NEW JERSEY

The curtain rises on a vast primitive wasteland, not unlike certain parts of New Jersey.

—Woody Allen, from "A Guide to Some of the Lesser
Ballets," in *Without Feathers*

. . . . .

NEW YORK

New York makes one think of the collapse of civilization, about Sodom and Gomorrah, the end of the world. The end wouldn't come as a surprise here. Many people already are banking on it.

—Saul Bellow

She always associated Babylon with New York, and she wished, now, that she lived in Manhattan, where one could die in a bright millisecond, without suffering, without risking the indignity of panic.

—Pat Frank, from *Alas, Babylon*

We shouldn't panic about the future because at this very moment there are 12,000 people who have all the answers to America's and the world's problems. Five are candidates and the rest are driving cabs in New York.

—Robert Orben, from *2400 Jokes to Brighten Your Speeches*

. . . . .

NIGHT

Here the prehuman dignity of night
Stands, as it was and will be again. Oh beautiful
Darkness and silence, the two eyes that see God. Great staring eyes.

—Robinson Jeffers, from "Black-Out"

. . . . .

NIHILISM

Our first work must be the annihilation of everything as it now exists. The old world must be destroyed and replaced by a new one. When you have freed your mind from fear of God, and that childish respect for the fiction of right, then, then all the remaining chains that bind you—property, marriage, morality, and justice—will snap asunder like threads.

—Mikhail Bakunin, from *God and the State*

Our nada who are in nada, nada be thy name thy kingdom nada thy will be nada in nada as it is in nada. Give us this nada our daily nada and nada us our nada as we nada our nadas and nada us not into nada but deliver us from nada; pues nada, hail nothing full of nothing, nothing is with thee.

—Ernest Hemingway, from *A Clean Well-Lighted Place*

. . . . .

NOISINESS

Enlil heard the clamor and he said to the gods in council, "The uproar of mankind is intolerable and sleep is no longer possible by reason of the Babel." So the gods agreed to exterminate mankind.

—from *The Epic of Gilgamesh*

. . . . .

NORMALCY

There will be wars and rumours of wars and all kinds of catastrophes, as there always are. Things will be, in that sense, normal, the hour before the heavens roll up like a scroll. You cannot guess it. If you could, one chief purpose for which it was foretold would be frustrated.

—C. S. Lewis, from *The World's Last Night*

Let it not enter the mind that anything in the world's system will cease to exist when the Messiah comes, or that any novelty

will be introduced into the scheme of the universe. The world
will go on, normal as always.

—Moses Maimonides, from *Principles of Faith*

And those who expected lightning and thunder
Are disappointed.
And those who expected signs and archangels' trumpets
Do not believe it is happening now.
As long as the sun and the moon are above,
As long as the bumblebee visits a rose,
As long as rosy infants are born
No one believes it is happening now.

—Czeslaw Milosz, from "A Song on the End
of the World"

. . . . .

NOSTRADAMUS
(MICHEL DE NOTREDAME)

*The French, sixteenth-century physician who was also the most cel-
ebrated astrologer and future-caster of his age, to say nothing of
being the creator of moisturizing creams in demand by the queens
of Europe. His* Centuries, *consisting of thousands of stanzas of
verse, comprise his chief prophecies, with a special emphasis on
forecasting shifting political alliances and upheavals. This work is
written in a language so cryptic that interpreting him has been a
cottage industry for hundreds of years. He was consulted by mon-
archs and scientists from all over a very jittery and highly supersti-
tious world and his powerful and poetical writing still attracts*

afficionados today. The following passages seem to be addressing apocalyptic themes.

In the year 1999, and seven months, from the sky will come the great King of Terror. He will bring to life the great king of the Mongols. Before and after war reigns happily.

The year of the great Seventh number accomplished; it will appear at the time of the games of slaughter. Not far from the age of the great Millennium when the dead will come out of their graves.

—Century X, quatrains 72 and 74, from *The Final Prophecies of Nostradamus* by Erika Cheetham

. . . . .

NOTHINGNESS

What is at the world's end, as at its beginning, is not the Nothingness which explains nothing, but God. And this end must not simply be equated with a cosmic catastrophe and the sudden end of human history. What is old, transient, imperfect, and evil will indeed be ended: but this end must be understood as ultimate completion and fulfillment.

—Hans Küng, from *Why I Am Still a Christian*

Eternal nothingness is O.K. if you're dressed for it.

—Woody Allen, from *Getting Even*

The earth, even, is like a flower, so soon
passeth it away. And yet this nothing
is the seed of all—the clear eye
of Heaven, where all the worlds appear.

—Wendell Berry, from "The Slip"

He was the most inconsiderate creature in that swarming mass
of mankind which for a brief space occupied the surface of the
earth; and he was almighty because he had wrenched from chaos
the secret of nothingness.

—Jean-Paul Sartre, from *The Flies*

Blow soon to never and never to twice
(blow life to isn't:blow death to was)
—all nothing's along our hugest home;
the most who die,the more we live.

—E. E. Cummings, from "what if a much of a
which of a wind"

There with vast wings across the canceled skies,
There in the sudden blackness the black pall
Of nothing, nothing, nothing—nothing at all.

—Archibald MacLeish, from "The End of the World"

· · · · ·

Nuclear Power: The Accidents

A two-pound turkey and a fifty-pound cranberry—that's Thanksgiving dinner at Three-Mile Island.

—Johnny Carson

· · · · ·

Nuclear War: The Book Adaptation

Nuclear weapons could bring about the Book of Revelation in a matter of hours; they could do it today. Of course, no dead will rise; nothing will be revealed (*nothing* meaning two things, the absence of everything and a thing called *nothing*). Events that we call "acts of God"—floods, earthquakes, eruptions—are flesh wounds compared to the human act of nuclear war: a million Hiroshimas.

—Martin Amis, from *Einstein's Monsters*

· · · · ·

Nuclear War: The Contemplation

Today every inhabitant of this planet must contemplate the day when this planet may no longer be habitable. Every man, woman, and child lives under a nuclear sword of Damocles, hanging by the slenderest of threads, capable of being cut at any moment by accident, or miscalculation, or madness.

—President John F. Kennedy, address at the
United Nations, Sept. 1961

. . . . . .

NUCLEAR WAR:
THE MARKETING OPPORTUNITY

AUDREY: I've read Stone's scenario and it's terrible.

PAUL: Why don't we let Paramount decide.

AUDREY: It's about nuclear war.

PAUL (*Into phone*): Hold on. (*To* AUDREY) Paramount will only consider projects about nuclear war if there's an upbeat ending.

—Arthur Kopit, from *End of the World*

The *Nuke* running shoe has a unique deep-waffle sole that gives you that extra spring you need to go from Ground Zero to Mile 20 in just five seconds. Break in a pair of *Nukes* today. You might be there to be glad you did.

—from *Meet Mr. Bomb: A Practical Guide
to Nuclear Extinction*

. . . . .

NUCLEAR WAR: THE MOMENT

She will see it rising, lifting up
over our horizon, the upper rim of the gold ball, large as a
        giant
planet starting to lift up over ours.
She will stand there in the yard holding her daughter,
looking at it rise and glow and blossom and rise,
and the child will open her arms to it,
it will look so beautiful.

> —Sharon Olds, from "When," in *The Gold Cell*

In the silent rush of hot wind, like the opening of a trillion
oven doors that you've been imagining since you were six, it's all
over.

> —Douglas Coupland, from *Generation X*

. . . . .

NUCLEAR WAR: SURVIVAL TIPS

Be sure to carry your credit cards, cash, checks, stocks, insur-
ance policies, and will. Every effort will be made to clear
trans–nuclear attack checks, including those drawn on destroyed
banks. You will be encouraged to buy U.S. Savings Bonds.

Following a nuclear attack on the United States, the U.S. Postal Service plans to distribute Emergency Change of Address Cards.

—directives from FEMA (Federal Emergency Management Agency), Executive Order #11490, 1969

Dig a hole, cover it with a couple of doors and then throw three feet of dirt on top. . . . It's the dirt that does it. . . . You know, dirt is just great stuff. . . . If there are enough shovels to go around, everybody's going to make it.

—Thomas K. Jones, quoted in *With Enough Shovels: Reagan, Bush and Nuclear War* by Robert Scheer

. . . . .

NUCLEAR WEAPONS: THE CHOICE

One day—and it is hard to believe it will not be soon—we will make our choice. Either we will sink into the final coma and end it all or, as I trust and believe, we will awaken to the truth of our peril, a truth as great as life itself . . . we will break through the layers of our denials, put aside our fainthearted excuses, and rise up to cleanse the earth of nuclear weapons.

—Jonathan Schell, from *The Fate of the Earth*

If somebody knows you have a nuclear weapon in your house, they're going to think twice about breaking in.

—Art Buchwald, from "The Hydrogen Bomb Lobby," in *Laid Back in Washington*

O

OBLITERATION

That Hiroshima was more sudden and more impersonal than Auschwitz, whatever other moral differences may be discerned, makes it none the less immoral. One should reflect carefully on how far they must be bracketed together in the record of moral insensibility and the deformation of humanity. By the time of Korea, at any rate, the principle of obliteration had become totally accepted as part of the moral universe of the mass society.

—C. Wright Mills, from *The Causes of World War Three*

. . . . .

OTHER LIFE

But who shall dwell in these worlds if they be inhabited? . . . Are we or they Lords of the World? . . . And how are things made for man?

—Johannes Kepler, quoted in *The Anatomy of Melancholy* by Robert Burton

Across the gulf of space, minds that are to our minds as ours are to those of the beasts that perish, intellects vast and cool and unsympathetic, regarded this earth with envious eyes, and slowly and surely drew their plans against us.

—H. G. Wells, from *The War of the Worlds*

. . . . .

OVERDUE

The good news is that the world's future is pregnant with possibilities. The bad news is, it's now in its 8,947,548th month.

—Robert Orben

. . . . .

OVERPOPULATION

There are more dead people than living, and their numbers are increasing.

—Eugene Ionesco, from *The Rhinoceros*

How can we help a foreign country to escape overpopulation? Clearly the worst thing we can do is send food. . . . Atomic bombs would be kinder. For a few moments the misery would be acute, but it would soon come to an end for most of the people, leaving a very few survivors.

—Garrett Hardin, in "The Immorality of Being Softhearted," from *Stanford Alumni* magazine, Jan. 1969

In every grave make room, make room!
The world's at an end, and we come, we come.

—Sir William Davenant, from "The Law
Against Lovers"

The continued growth in the number of people who inhabit this planet will inevitably increase the substantial damage that the atmosphere, the water table and the arable soil have already suffered.

—from "A Call to Reason," signed by 87 Nobel
Laureates in support of the International Conference
on Population and Development, from the *New York
Times*, Aug. 30, 1994

Ideal mankind would abolish death, multiply itself million upon million, rear up city upon city, save every parasite alive, until the accumulation of mere existence is swollen to a horror.

—D. H. Lawrence, from *St. Mawr*

. . . . .

OVERPRODUCTION

Indeed, provisions will be so cheap upon earth that people will imagine that peace is assured for them, and then calamities shall spring up on the earth—the sword, famine, and great confusion.

—2 Esdras 16:21

P

PAIN

Now as we keep our watch and await the final day, count no mortal happy till he dies, free of pain at last.

—Sophocles, from *King Oedipus*

It is astonishing how such a simple and commonplace ailment as pain and nausea can knock everything else out of one's head, lofty thoughts, profound thoughts, crazy thoughts, even lust.

Ooooooh, he groaned aloud.

Let me out of here, he said, with no thought of God, Jews, suicide, tigers, or the Last Days.

—Walker Percy, from *The Second Coming*

. . . . .

PANIC

All you need do is just to threaten your neighbor with any of the weapons of mass destruction. Their own panic will do the rest. . . . Not a shot had been fired and civilization was already in ruins.

—Aldous Huxley, from *Ape and Essence*

. . . . .

PARADISE

I have always imagined that Paradise will be a kind of library.

—Jorge Luis Borges

. . . . .

PARADOX

Humanity adores only those who cause it to perish.

—E. M. Cioran, from *A Short History of Decay*

. . . . .

PEACEABLE KINGDOM

The wolf shall live with the lamb, the leopard shall lie down with the kid, the calf and the lion and the fatling together and a little child shall lead them.

—Isaiah 11:6

No absolute is going to make the lion lay down with the lamb unless the lamb is inside.

—D. H. Lawrence

And the lion and the calf shall lie down together, but the calf won't get much sleep.

—Woody Allen, from "The Scrolls," in
Without Feathers

. . . . .

PERFUME

The approaching end of the world strikes me like some obvious but quite subtle scent—just as a traveler nearing the sea feels the sea breeze before he sees the sea.

—Vladimir Solovyev

. . . . .

PERSPECTIVE

"My friend," said the orator, "do you believe that the Pope is Anti-Christ?" "I had never heard so before," said Candide, "but whether he is or isn't I am starving."

—Voltaire, from *Candide*

If there were a plant in your hand, and they should say to you: Look, the messiah is here! Go and plant your plant first, and after that go forth to receive them.

—Rabbi Johanan

Somehow the world never manages to end before your homework is due. Also, if the world's about to end, why aren't things more interesting? Why are people abandoning themselves to cares and gripes instead of to booze-ups and orgies? Why aren't I having an affair with Ava Gardner the way Gregory Peck was in *On the Beach?*

—P. J. O'Rourke, from *All the Trouble in the World*

Taking a very gloomy view of the future of the human race, let us suppose that it can only expect to survive for two thousand million years longer, a period about equal to the past age of the earth. Then, regarded as a being destined to live for three-score years and ten, humanity, although it has been born in a house seventy years old, is itself only three days old.

—Sir James Jeans, from *Eos*

. . . . .

PEYOTE

When the world ends, it will be like when the names of things are changed, during the peyote hunt. All will be different, the opposite of what it is now. Now there are two eyes in the heavens, *Dios Sol* and *Dios Fuego*. Then, the moon will open his eye and become brighter. The sun will become dimmer. There will be no more difference. No more man and woman. No child and no adult. All will change places.

> —Huichol Indian myth, from "Peyote and the Mystic
> Vision" by Barbara Myerhoff, in *Art of the
> Huichol Indians*

. . . . .

PLAGUE

God is deaf now-a-days and deigneth not hear us, / And prayers have no power the Plague to stay.

> —William Langland, from *Piers Plowman*

And no bells tolled, and nobody wept no matter what his loss because almost everyone expected death. . . . And people said and believed, "This is the end of the world."

> —Agnolo di Tura, on the Plague in Siena, quoted in *A
> Distant Mirror: The Calamitous 14th Century* by
> Barbara W. Tuchman

Imagine a virus [such as Ebola] with the infectiousness of influenza and the mortality rate of the Black Plague in the Middle Ages.

—Richard Preston, from *The Hot Zone*

. . . . .

POLITICAL CORRECTNESS

The six horsemen of the politically correct apocalypse—overpopulation, famine, ecological disaster, ethnic hatred, plague, and poverty.

—Florence King, in her review of *All the Trouble in the World*, by P. J. O'Rourke, in the *New York Times*, Oct. 16, 1994

If the last Jewish liberals cannot get it through their brains that affirmative action is nothing less than the end of civilization as we know it, then maybe it's time for a collective lobotomy. With their luck, it would be performed by a quota-ordained neurosurgeon.

—Hilly Gross, in *Jewish Week*, March 24, 1995

. . . . .

POLITICS

One of the most versatile features of the apocalyptic genre is that a good apocalypse uses prophetic visions—made in the past—not only to prophesy the future but also to explain, justify, and reveal purported truths behind current events and, in the process, to forecast the immediate or hoped-for political future. While this offers comfort, release, or at least a sense of order and direction to apocalypse-followers, who, like the early Christians, have often been marginal or persecuted, apocalypse reading and rhetoric are also employed by the politically powerful.

So when there shall appear in the world earthquakes, tumult of peoples, intrigues of nations, wavering of leaders, confusion of princes, then you will know.

—2 Esdras 9:3–4

In last Sunday's debate, the president [Ronald Reagan] said "no one knows whether Armageddon is a thousand years away or day after tomorrow."

—from an editorial in the *New York Times*,
Oct. 25, 1984

We stand at Armageddon, and we battle for the Lord!

—Theodore Roosevelt, at the Bull Moose party
convention, Chicago, 1912, as quoted in
Safire's New Political Dictionary

We now face the ultimate political powershift. We can re-design democracy for the 21st century—or descend into a new Dark Age.
One path moves power from the state toward the individual. The other threatens to shrink the individual to zero.

—Alvin Toffler, from *Powershift*

"Well, what about this: in *Revelation*, it says he [Antichrist] shall rise from the eternal sea. . . . And theologians have already interpreted the eternal sea as meaning the world of politics. . . ."

"So the devil's child will rise from the world of politics?"

—from *The Omen*, film written by David Seltzer,
directed by Richard Donner

If the question could be put to a popular vote, I do not believe a single state would vote for the coming of Jesus to reign here as he reigns in Heaven. I do not believe a single county, city, ward in this city, or a single precinct in this country would vote for His coming . . . the Republican party would vote for the biggest blackguard on earth rather than for Him. The Democrats would vote solidly against Him. Even the Prohibitionists wouldn't want Him here. I see some of you shaking your heads. Well, shake 'em. I'm talking facts.

—Dwight L. Moody, in the *New York Times*,
March 21, 1898

. . . . .

POLLUTION

We are close to dead. There are faces and bodies like gorged maggots on the dance floor, on the highway, in the city, in the stadium; they are a host of chemical machines who swallow the products of chemical factories, aspirin, preservatives, stimulant, relaxant, and breathe out their chemical wastes into a polluted air. The sense of a long last night over civilization is back again.

—Norman Mailer, from "Introducing Our Argument"
in *Cannibals and Christians*

Now I am terrified at the Earth, it is that calm and
    patient,
It turns harmless and stainless on its axis, with such
    endless successions of diseas'd corpses
It distills such exquisite winds out of such infused fetor,
It renews with such unwitting looks its prodigal, annual,
    sumptuous crops,
It gives such divine materials to men, and accepts such
    leavings from them at last.

—Walt Whitman, from "This Compost"

. . . . .

PREDICTIONS

Citing year, day, and even the hour of the End seems to be especially important to groups on the fringe, turning up as it does among the early Christians, among the most radical Protestants of the Reformation era, and, in our own time, among groups such as the Jehovah's Witnesses and the Seventh-Day Adventists and their offshoot, the Branch Davidians. However, as Christians gained converts, influence, and power, there was a lot more world to lose by projecting a date for universal destruction. As a result, in the Christian mainstream, as represented by St. Augustine, for example, universal destruction was gradually spiritualized, internalized as a personal fate to avoid within each human heart, and in various ways put on the theological back burner. Nevertheless, dissidents as well as new and emerging sects continue to find calculating and predicting the End an effective recruiting and rallying strategy, and one which often remains effective even as predictions fail and the sun continues to shine.

We were living the last days, a tale already told.

—Ruth Riddle, a Branch Davidian follower at Waco,
on *Turning Point*, Aug. 3, 1994

There have been endtimes aplenty in the six thousand years of recorded history, but never one so universal or so dangerous. Only the demon of relativism bars us from full consciousness of our predicament. Be not deceived. Our twentieth-century endtime does surpass, in scope and destructive potential, all others.

—Warren Wagar, from *Terminal Visions: The
Literature of Last Things*

. . . . .

PREMILLENNIALISM

Currently the most popular and influential apocalyptic model among American fundamentalists, it was put on the evangelical map by J. N. Darby in 1875, and the turn-of-the-century preacher Dwight Moody—the Billy Graham of his era—popularized it. Now, with varying debate over details, it is espoused by the household names of the religious right as a guide to find a literal fulfillment for the prophecies of the Bible. The premillennial forecast is a breathless scenario worthy of a Hollywood adventure film—during the rise of which as a form of entertainment it, incidentally, took shape. It is ignited by the Rapture, that sudden ascent to heaven of the faithful believers in the seconds before the first earthquakes strike, then followed by the Tribulation with its wars, famines, and so forth, and the engagement of Antichrist and his capture in the pit for a thousand years. The ensuing blissful Millennium is reigned over by the returned Jesus, is capped by one last gasp of a final battle, judgment and reward, and then the earth is burned to a crisp and supplanted by a new heaven on earth for the surviving believers.

I believe the settlement of those Russian and European Jews [in Israel] is critical to the fulfillment of prophecy. Personally, I always like to cooperate with prophecy, not fight it! If God has a purpose—as He certainly does in Israel—we don't want to be seen as opposing it.

—Pat Robertson, from *The Secret Kingdom*

Because it is part of a long intellectual tradition with extensive and systematic content, it [premillennial thought] deserves to be accorded serious examination, not to be dismissed as nonsense.

—William Martin, from "Waiting for the End," in *The Atlantic Monthly,* June 1982

. . . . .

PROGRESS AND TECHNOLOGY

Progress might have been all right once, but it has gone on too long.

—Ogden Nash

Although personally I am quite content with existing explosives, I feel we must not stand in the way of improvement.

—Sir Winston Churchill, from *The Second World War*
in reference to the possibility of making a
nuclear bomb

Just consider what they were up to during the century and a half before the Thing. Fouling the rivers, killing off the wild animals, destroying the forests, washing the topsoil into the sea, burning up an ocean of petroleum, squandering the minerals it had taken the whole of ecological time to deposit. An orgy of criminal imbecility. And they called it Progress.

—Aldous Huxley, from *Ape and Essence*

Intensified progress seems to be bound up with intensified unfreedom. Concentration camps, mass exterminations, world wars, and atom bombs are no "relapse into barbarism," but the unrepressed implementation of the achievements of modern science, technology, and domination.

—Herbert Marcuse, from *Eros and Civilization*

Of so much haste, of so much impatience, our machines are the consequence and not the cause. It is not they that are driving civilized man to his doom: rather he has invented them because he was already on his way there; he sought means, auxiliaries, to attain it faster and more effectively. Not content to run, he preferred to *ride* to perdition.

—E. M. Cioran, from *The Fall into Time*

. . . . .

PROPHECY

Fear prophets . . . and those prepared to die for the truth, for as a rule they make many others die with them, often before them, at times instead of them.

—Umberto Eco, quoted in *Expect the Worst,*
Eric Marcus, ed.

In every man sleeps a prophet, and when he wakes there is a little more evil in the world.

—E. M. Cioran, from *A Short History of Decay*

God gave . . . the Prophecies of the Old Testament, not to gratify men's curiosities by enabling them to foreknow things, but that after they were fulfilled they might be interpreted by the event, and his own Providence, not the Interpreters, be then manifested thereby to the world.

—Sir Isaac Newton, from *Observations upon the*
Prophecies of Daniel, and the Apocalypse of St. John

Prophecy today is hardly the romantic business that it used to be. The old tools of the trade, like the sword, the hair shirt, and the long fast in the wilderness have given way to more contemporary, mundane instructions of doom—the book, the picket and petition, the sit-in at City Hall.

—Jane Kramer, from "The Ranks and Rungs of Mrs.
Jacobs' Ladder," in *Off Washington Square*

Nor shall you scare us with talk of the
death of the race
How should we dream of this place without us?—
The sun mere fire, the leaves untroubled about us
A stone look on the stone's face.

—Richard Wilbur, from "Advice to a Prophet"

I always avoid prophesying beforehand, because it is a much better policy to prophesy after the event has already taken place.

—Sir Winston Churchill, speaking at a Cairo press
conference, Feb. 2, 1943

Beware that you are not led astray; for many will come in my name and say, "I am He!" and "The time is near!" Do not go after them.

—Luke 21:8

. . . . .

PSYCHOLOGY

"I have a theory. You want to hear it? The human race is having a nervous breakdown!"

> —from *Adam's Rib*, film written by Ruth Gordon and
> Garson Kanin, directed by George Cukor

. . . . .

PUNISHMENT

We are heading towards catastrophe. I think the world is going to pieces. I am very pessimistic. Why? Because the world hasn't been punished yet, and the only punishment that could be adequate is the nuclear destruction of the world.

> —Elie Wiesel, interviewed in *Writers at Work*,
> George Plimpton, ed.

It is an open question whether any behavior based on the fear of eternal punishment can be regarded as ethical or should be regarded as merely cowardly.

> —Margaret Mead, quoted in *Redbook* magazine,
> Feb. 1971

Eternal punishment for the wicked finds no official acceptance in Judaism. There were few Rabbis indeed who entertained the violent views of the Apocalypses on this subject. The

Mishna, which contains only scant reference to Gehenna, limits the punishment of the wicked to twelve months.

—Abba Hillel Silver, from *Where Judaism Differs*

A material resurrection seems strange and even absurd except for purposes of punishment, and all punishment which is to revenge rather than correct must be morally wrong, and when the World is at an end, what moral or warning purpose can eternal tortures answer?

—Lord Byron, from *Detached Thoughts*

R

RACE

If we—and now I mean the relatively conscious whites and the relatively conscious blacks, who must, like lovers, insist on, or create, the consciousness of others—do not falter in our duty now, we may be able, handful that we are, to end the racial nightmare, and achieve our country, and change the history of the world. If we do not now dare everything, the fulfillment of that prophecy, re-created from the Bible in song by a slave, is upon us: *God gave Noah the rainbow sign, No more water, the fire next time!*

—James Baldwin, from *The Fire Next Time*

Some Negroes who believe the resurrection think that they shall rise white.

—Thomas Browne, from *Christian Morals*

. . . . .

RAPTURE

The taking up of the faithful, each in his or her own dazzling spiritual elevator, straight up into heaven. This is a miraculous event, believers think, which will occur right before the Millennium, and also before, or, according to other interpretations, during the Tribulation, which is the period of upheavals of war, disease, and natural disaster that herald the ushering in of these last things.

For the Lord himself, with a cry of command, with the archangel's call and with the sound of God's trumpet, will descend from heaven, and the dead in Christ will rise first. Then we who are alive, who are left, will be caught up in the clouds together with them to meet the Lord in the air.

—1 Thessalonians 4:16–17

Then two will be in the field; one will be taken and one will be left. Two women will be grinding meal together; one will be taken and one will be left. Keep awake therefore, for you do not know on what day your Lord is coming.

—Matthew 24:40–42

"If you're a Christian and you're ironing your shirts and the Rapture happens, you get taken up to heaven in the middle of doing your laundry, do you turn off the iron or do your shirts burn?"

"I wear permanent press."

—dialogue between a believer and a nonbeliever, from *The Rapture*, film written and directed by Mike Tolkin

Jesus our Savior is a-coming to reign
And take you up to glory in His aeroplane.
There will be no punctures or muddy roads
No broken axles from overloads,
No shocks to give trouble or cause delay
As we soon will rapture up the narrow way.

—Anonymous, from "The Heavenly Aeroplane,"
folk song

. . . . .

REAGAN, RONALD

I believe that Ronald Reagan can make this country what it once was—an arctic region covered with ice.

—Steve Martin (attributed)

. . . . .

REAL ESTATE

The universe is merely a fleeting idea in God's mind—a pretty uncomfortable thought, particularly if you've just made a down payment on a house.

—Woody Allen, from *Getting Even*

. . . . .

REASON

Reason is natural revelation, whereby the eternal Father of light, and fountain of all knowledge communicates to mankind that portion of truth which he has laid within the reach of their natural faculties.

—John Locke, from *An Essay concerning Human Understanding*

The unleashed power of the atom has changed everything save our modes of thinking and we thus drift toward unparalleled catastrophe.

—Albert Einstein, in telegram to prominent Americans, in the *New York Times*, May 25, 1946

Cogito ergo boom.

—Susan Sontag, from *Styles of Radical Will*

It is not contrary to reason to prefer the destruction of the whole world to the scratching of my finger.

—David Hume, from A *Treatise Upon Human Nature*

. . . . .

RECAPPING

Do not regard the order of what is said [in the book of Revelation] because the sevenfold Holy Spirit, when he has run through matters down to the last moment of time and the end, returns again to the same times [?] and completes what he has left unsaid.

—Victorinus of Pettau, from *Commentary on Revelation 8:2–3* in "Revelation," Bernard McGinn, trans., from *The Literary Guide to the Bible*, Frank Kermode and Robert Alter, eds.

. . . . .

RECOLLAPSING

The present evidence therefore suggests that the universe will probably expand forever, but all we can really be sure of is that even if the universe is going to recollapse, it won't do so for at least another ten thousand million years, since it has already been expanding for at least that long. This should not unduly worry us: by that time, unless we have colonized beyond the Solar System, mankind will long since have died out, extinguished along with our sun!

—Stephen Hawking, from *A Brief History of Time*

. . . . .

REDEMPTION

For I came not to judge the world but to save the world.

—John 12:47

It is good that one should wait quietly for the salvation of the Lord.

—Lamentations 3:26

The Lubavitch Rebbe Has Declared
The Time of the Redemption Has Arrived
To learn more, please call:
718 2 MOSHIACH 7

—from an advertisement in the *Jewish Week,*
Jan. 14, 1994

. . . . .

REFRESHMENT OF THE SAINTS

A doctrine teaching that God rewards—some would say avenges—his saints, the particularly pious people, and the martyrs, not only through resurrection into heaven, but also with a period of time for them to live high on the hog here on earth during the Millennium, that is, before the general resurrection. The interpretations of the early heresiarch, Montanus, might have contributed to the development of this idea.

I also saw the souls of those who had been beheaded for their testimony to Jesus. . . . They had not worshipped the beast or its image and had not received its mark on their forehead or their hands. They came to life and reigned with Christ a thousand years. (The rest of the dead did not come to life until the thousand years were ended.)

—Revelation, 20:4–5

In Judea for forty days there was a city suspended from the sky at the break of morning . . . the whole fashion of the ramparts faded out as day advanced, and at other times it suddenly disappeared. This city, we affirm, has been provided by God for the reception of the saints by resurrection, and for their refreshment with abundance of all blessings—spiritual ones—in compensation for those which in this world we have either refused or been denied. For it is both just, and worthy of God, that his servants should also have joy in that place where they have suffered affliction in his name.

—Tertullian, from *Adversus Marionem*

. . . . .

REPRIEVE

I will never again curse the ground because of humankind, for the inclination of the human heart is evil from youth. . . . As long as the earth endures, seedtime and harvest, cold and heat, summer and winter, day and night, shall not cease.

—Genesis 8:21–22

The sun rose this morning at 6:32 A.M. This gratifying event was first reported by Mrs. Dorothy Stetson of Freeport, Long Island, who promptly telephoned the mayor. The Society for Affirming the End of the World at once went into a special session and postponed the arrival of that event for twenty-four hours. All honor to Mrs. Stetson for her public spirit.

—Thornton Wilder, from *The Skin of Our Teeth*

. . . . .

RESTRAINING FORCE

An apocalyptic idea that grew particularly popular after Rome became officially Christian, it was devised in order to explain the continuing delay in the return of Jesus and the articulation of the endtime events. Using the prophecies in Daniel and other texts, medieval theologians explained that the evolving secular kingdoms were still the descendants of Rome; as long as they were in place, they restrained the endtime events from triggering. As late as the English Civil War, for example, radicals in the Puritan armies, known as the Fifth Monarchy Men, were instrumental in the execution of Charles I. They claimed he was the Beast, and his the fourth kingdom—of iron—from the biblical visions, which had to be eliminated, thus removing the final restraining obstacle to the inauguration of the never-ending millennial kingdom as foretold.

Hence the Apostle Paul says that Antichrist will not come into the world unless first comes the falling-away, that is, unless first all kingdoms fall away from the Roman empire to which they were long subject. This time has not yet come, because though we see the Roman empire destroyed in great part, nevertheless as long as the kings of the Franks . . . shall last, the dignity of the Roman empire will not totally perish.

—from "Adso's Letter on the Antichrist,"
D. Verhelst, trans.

As to the coming of our Lord Jesus Christ . . . let no one deceive you in any way; for that day will not come unless the rebellion comes first and the lawless one is revealed. . . .

And you know what is now restraining him, so that he may be revealed when his time comes.

—2 Thessalonians 2:1–6

. . . . .

RESURRECTION

But at that time your people shall be delivered, everyone who is found written in the book. Many of those who sleep in the dust of the earth shall awake, some to everlasting life, and some to shame and everlasting contempt.

—Daniel 12:1–2

If there is no resurrection of the dead, then Christ has not been raised; and if Christ has not been raised, then our proclamation has been in vain and your faith has been in vain. . . . Then those also who have died in Christ have perished. If for this life only we have hoped in Christ, we are of all people most to be pitied.

—1 Corinthians 15:13–19

Belief in the Messiah and in the resurrection of the dead are principles peculiar to Christianity which cannot be conceived without them. But resurrection and the Messiah [in Judaism] are like branches issuing from the principles of Reward and Punishment and are not root principles in themselves.

—Joseph Albo, from the *Book of Roots*

Surely death is not death, and humanity is not extinct; but merely passed into other shapes, unsubjected to our perceptions. Death is a vast portal, a high road to life: let us hasten to pass; let us exist no more in this living death, but die that we may live!

—Mary Shelley, from *The Last Man*

The world dies over and over again, but the skeleton always gets up and walks.

—Henry Miller, from "Uterine Hunger" in
The Wisdom of the Heart

Do not be astonished at this; for the hour is coming when all who are in their graves will hear his voice and will come out—those who have done good, to the resurrection of life, and those who have done evil, to the resurrection of condemnation.

—John 5:28–29

. . . . .

Resurrection: Body and Soul

So there are two resurrections—the one the first and spiritual resurrection, which has place in this life and preserves us from coming into the second death; the other the second, which does not occur now, but in the end of the world, and which is of the body, not of the soul, and which by the last judgment shall dismiss some into the second death, others into that life which has no death. . . .

. . . The evangelist John has spoken of these two resurrections in the book which is called the Apocalypse, but in such a way that some Christians do not understand the first of the two and so construe the passage into ridiculous fancies.

—St. Augustine, from *City of God*

. . . . .

RESURRECTION: THE BONES

Then he said to me, "Prophesy to these bones, and say to them: O dry bones, hear the word of the Lord. Thus says the Lord God to these bones: I will cause breath to enter you, and you shall live. I will lay sinews on you, and will cause flesh to come upon you, and cover you with skin, and put breath in you, and you shall live. . . . I prophesied as he commanded me, and the breath came into them, and they lived, and stood on their feet, a vast multitude.

—Ezekiel 37:4–6, 10

. . . . .

RESURRECTION: MISTAKEN

That night your great guns, unawares,
Shook all our coffins as we lay,
And broke the chancel window-squares,
We thought it was the Judgment-day.

. . . The glebe cow drooled. Till God called, "No";
It's gunnery practice out at sea

Just as before you went below;
The world is as it used to be.

—Thomas Hardy, from "Channel Firing"

. . . . .

RESURRECTION: MOON

The moon dies and comes back to life again. She said to the hare, "Go to man and say to him: 'Just as I die and return to life, so should you die and become alive again.'"

The hare came to man and said: "Just as I die and do not return to life, so must you die and not come back to life." When he returned the moon said: "What message did you give to man?" "I said to him: 'Just as I die and do not return to life so must you die and not come back to life.'"

"What!" cried the moon. "You told him that?" And she took a stick and hit him on the mouth, splitting it open.

—"The Origin of Death," an African (Hottentot) tale,
rendered by Blaise Cendrars

. . . . .

RESURRECTION: SEX

Some say that women shall not rise again in the female sex, but all in the male; but they seem to me wiser who have no hesitation in affirming that all shall rise again in their own sex.

—St. Augustine, from *City of God*

. . . . .

REVELATION: THE BOOK

Revelation has as many mysteries as it does words.

—St. Jerome

I have read the Book of Revelation and yes, I believe the world is going to end—by an act of God, I hope—but every day I think that time is running out.

—Caspar Weinberger, interviewed in the *New York Times*, Aug. 23, 1982

It is between fifty and sixty years since I read the Apocalypse, and I then considered it merely the ravings of a lunatic.

—Thomas Jefferson

A curious record of the visions of a drug addict.

—George Bernard Shaw

Revelation, n: A famous book in which St. John the Divine concealed all that he knew. The revealing is done by the commentators, who know nothing.

—Ambrose Bierce, from *The Devil's Dictionary*

If you listen to the Salvation Army you will hear that they are going to be very grand. Very grand indeed, since they get to heaven. *Then* they'll show you what's what. Then you'll be put in your place, you superior person, you Babylon: down in hell and brimstone.

This is entirely the tone of Revelation.

—D. H. Lawrence, from *Apocalypse*

. . . . .

REVENGE

A recurrent leitmotif in much apocalyptic thinking, revenge—in the form of awesome destruction, judgment, or missing out on resurrection—is exacted on the outsiders, the evil ones, heretics, Jews, nonbelievers, persecutors, or whoever fits the bill at a given historical moment. The with-us-or-against-us moral absolutism that underlies apocalyptic revenge may derive from the bloody persecutions experienced by the early Christians, who wrote the pattern-setting apocalypses.

When they [the righteous] see themselves besieged, they will call loudly to God for help. . . . Then the heavens shall be opened in a tempest, and Christ shall descend with great power . . . and all that multitude of the godless shall be annihilated, and torrents of blood shall flow.

—Lactantius

I call Christianity the one great curse, the one enormous and innermost perversion, the one great instinct of revenge, for which no means are too venomous, too underhand, too underground and too petty—I call it the one immortal blemish of mankind.

—Friedrich Nietzsche, from *The Antichrist*

Drive Christ's enemies out from among the Elect, for you are the instruments for that purpose. . . . If they resist, let them be slaughtered without mercy.

—Thomas Munzer, from his sermons

And the Apocalypse [that is, Revelation] . . . is repellent because it resounds with the dangerous snarl of the frustrated, suppressed collective self, the frustrated power-spirit in man, vengeful.

—D. H. Lawrence, from *Apocalypse*

. . . . .

REVOLUTION

Compounded of great emotional urgency and the highest moral authority, apocalyptic vision and rhetoric have often been harnessed, both among the marginal or destitute and the powerful, to muster political and social revolt.

Here, my beloved brethren, he [Lord Grenville] brings forth the Stamp Act, that mark of slavery. . . . I beseech you then to beware as good christians and lovers of your country, lest by touching any paper with his impression, you received the mark of the beast.

—from an address given to the Sons of Liberty, Feb. 1776

The industrial revolution and its consequences have been a disaster for the human race. We therefore advocate a revolution against the industrial system. . . . Its object will be to overthrow not governments but the economic and technological basis of present society.

> —the "Unabomber," from "Industrial Society and
> Its Future"

We are not to weep as the people of the world weep when there are certain tragedies or breakups of the government or the systems of the world. We are not to wring our hands and say, "Isn't it awful?" That isn't awful at all. It's good. That is a token, an evident token of our salvation, of where God is going to take us.

> —Pat Robertson, as quoted in "Waiting for the End" by
> William Martin, in *The Atlantic Monthly*, June 1982

This war no longer bears the characteristics of former inter-European conflicts. It is one of those elemental conflicts that usher in a new millennium and which shake the world once in a thousand years.

> —Adolph Hitler, in a speech to the Reichstag,
> April 1942

I can imagine no man who will look with more horror on the End than a conscientious revolutionary who has, in a sense sincerely, been justifying cruelties and injustices inflicted on millions of his contemporaries by the benefits which he hopes to confer on future generations: generations who, as one terrible moment now reveals to him, were never going to exist.

> —C. S. Lewis, from *The World's Last Night*

. . . . .

ROCK AND ROLL

One o' these days 'bout twelve o'clock,
This ole worl' gonna reel an' rock;
I'm gonna leave, I'm gonna ride,
Six white horses side by side.

—American Negro song, quoted in *Wings on My Feet*
by H. W. Odum

The human race was dying out
No one left to scream and shout
People walking on the moon
Smog will get you pretty soon.

—The Doors, from "Ship of Fools"

. . . . .

ROME

While stands the Colosseum, Rome shall stand;
When falls the Colosseum, Rome shall fall;
And when Rome falls—the world.

—Lord Byron, from *Childe Harold's Pilgrimage*

. . . . .

ROTTING

You're either among the wicked or among the saved. The wicked get to rot as they walk down the street. They get to feel their own eyes slide out of their sockets. You'll know them by their stickiness and lost parts. People tracking slime of their own making. All the flashiness of Armageddon is in the rotting. The saved know each other by their neatness and reserve. He doesn't have showy ways is how you know a saved person.

—Don DeLillo, from *White Noise*

. . . . .

RWANDA

This is the beginning of the final days. This is the apocalypse.

—Deogracias Bivunde, a resident of Goma, Zaire, on witnessing the trampling to death of refugees on the Rwandan border. Quoted in *Time*, Aug. 1, 1994

In fact the world may end the way Rwanda is, person by person. . . . Who needs the Bomb when there are machetes and clubs?

—Roger Rosenblatt, from "End of the World," on *The MacNeil-Lehrer NewsHour*, Aug. 1994

S

SAINTS

In early Christian times, when apocalypse-writing flourished, saints were felt to be a holy and "alive" component of the community, a kind of ascendant counterpart complementing the yet earthbound community. The 144,000 saints of Revelation have long been interpreted by premillennialists to be Jews who earn their heavenly status by proclaiming Jesus their messiah and then suffering martyrdom as the battles of the last days unfold in Jerusalem.

Saints should always be judged guilty until they are proved innocent.

—George Orwell, from "Reflections on Gandhi," in
Shooting an Elephant

"I will be a saint" means I will despoil myself of all that is not God; I will strip my heart of all created things; I will live in poverty and detachment; I will renounce my will, my inclinations, my whims and fancies, and make myself a willing slave to the will of God.

—Mother Teresa in "Willing Slaves to the Will of God," from *A Gift to God*

. . . . .

SAINTS: FIREPROOFING

Someone will perhaps put the question, If after judgment is pronounced the world itself is to burn, where shall the saints be during the conflagration and before it is replaced by a new heaven and a new earth, since somewhere they must be, because they have material bodies. We may reply that they shall be in the upper regions into which the flame of that conflagration shall not ascend, as neither did the water of the flood.

—St. Augustine, from *City of God*

. . . . .

SAINTS: 144,000

Then I looked and there was the Lamb, standing on Mount Zion! And with him were one hundred forty-four thousand who had his name and his Father's name written on their foreheads. . . . It is these who have not defiled themselves with women, for they are virgins; these follow the Lamb wherever he goes. They have been redeemed from humankind.

—Revelation 14:1–4

Yamaiuchi was a Jehovah's Witness. He believed he was one of the 144,000 who would survive Armageddon and actually live in their bodies on this earth for a thousand years—and reign.

Yamaiuchi's wife . . . believed in reincarnation. She believed she had once been a priestess on Atlantis before it sank.

Is this an age of belief, he reflected, a great renaissance of faith after a period of crass materialism, atheism, agnosticism, liberalism, scientism? Or is it an age of madness in which everyone believes everything? Which?

The only unbelievers he knew . . . were even more demented than the believers.

—Walker Percy, from *The Second Coming*

. . . . .

SALVATION

Human salvation lies in the hands of the creatively maladjusted.

—Martin Luther King, from *Strength to Love*

When you have understood that nothing *is*, that things do not even deserve the status of appearances, you no longer need to be saved, you are saved, and miserable for it.

—E. M. Cioran, from "Encounters with Suicide," in *The New Gods*

That well-grounded system which tends to man's salvation, namely our faith, which, received from the church, we hold, and which always, through the Spirit of God, renews its youth, like some extraordinary deposit in an excellent vessel, and causes the very vessel in which it is to renew its youth.

—Iraneus, from *Against Heresy*

The salvation of this human world lies nowhere else than in the human heart, in the human power to reflect, in human meekness and human responsibility.

—Vaclav Havel, quoted in *International Herald Tribune*, Feb. 21, 1990

Can You Spare 12 Hours to Save Christians from Destruction?

—Christian Coalition recruitment brochure copy, quoted in "Christian Soldiers," by Sidney Blumenthal, in *The New Yorker*, July 18, 1994

The savior who wants to turn men into angels is as much a hater of human nature as the totalitarian despot who wants to turn them into puppets.

—Eric Hoffer, from *Reflections on the Human Condition*

· · · · ·

SAME TIME TOMORROW

JON: Shall we compose ourselves then?
PETER: Good plan. Prepare for the end of the world. Fifteen seconds!

DUDLEY: Here, have you got the picnic basket?

ALAN: Yes.

PETER: Five, four, three, two, one, zero!

ALL:

> Now is the end,
> Perish the world!

PETER: It was G.M.T. [Greenwich Mean Time], wasn't it?

JON: Yes.

PETER: Well, it's not quite the conflagration we'd been banking on. Never mind, lads, same time tomorrow, we must get a winner one day.

—from *Beyond the Fringe,* by Alan Bennett, Peter Cook, Jonathan Miller, and Dudley Moore

. . . . .

SAN FRANCISCO

The strong eschatology factions in San Francisco convince the population every three months that the end has come. The natives then parade with tapers through the streets toward Golden Gate Park where they make music with their eyes turned toward the heavens. A small percentage of worldenders remains convinced that the world has indeed ended and, over the years, they've begun to amount to a voting block. Mayoral candidates like Jesus Christ Satan always get 8 to 12 percent.

—Andrei Codrescu, from *In America's Shoes*

. . . . .

SCANDAL

The day the world ends, no one will be there, just as no one was there when it began. This is a scandal. Such a scandal for the human race that it is indeed capable collectively, out of spite, of hastening the end of the world by all means, just so it can enjoy the show.

—Jean Baudrillard, from *Cool Memories*

. . . . .

SCIENCE

Life is extinct on other planets because their scientists were more advanced than ours.

—Unknown

The greater the scientific advance, the more primitive the fear.

—Don DeLillo, from *White Noise*

The usual approach of science of constructing a mathematical model cannot answer the questions of why there should be a universe for the model to describe. Why does the universe go to all the bother of existing? Is the unified theory so compelling that it brings about its own existence?

—Stephen Hawking, from *A Brief History of Time*

. . . . .

SCIENCE FICTION

A generation that learns its magic from Tom Swift or Jules Verne has a much more optimistic outlook than one that is constantly being told that the planet is dying and that everything humanity is doing is wrong.

—Newt Gingrich, quoted in the *New York Review of Books*, Aug. 10, 1995

Earth is gone. . . . Even if there hadn't been a war we would have come to Mars, I think. . . . Now, of course—"

—Ray Bradbury, from *The Martian Chronicles*

In [science fiction films] it is by means of images and sounds, not words that have to be translated by the imagination, that one can participate in the fantasy of living through one's own death and more, the death of cities, the destruction of humanity itself.

—Susan Sontag, from "The Imagination of Disaster," in *Against Interpretation*

. . . . .

THE SEA

For all at last return to the sea—to Oceanus, the ocean river, like the ever-flowing stream of time, the beginning of the end.

—Rachel Carson

. . . . .

SECOND COMING

The doctrine of the actual return of Jesus is the sine qua non, the indispensable link in the chain that runs to the End as conceived by traditional Christianity. However, according to Origen, St. Augustine, and other early Church innovators, Jesus' return was to be seen not as physical but as the spiritual reemergence of Christ in the souls of the devout. This dichotomy—individual spiritual conversion versus worldwide physical cleansing—remains a fundamental difference among many Christians.

But in those days, after that suffering, the sun will be darkened, and the moon will not give its light, and the stars will be falling from heaven, and the powers in the heavens will be shaken. Then they will see the Son of Man coming in clouds with great power and glory. Then he will send out the angels, and gather his elect from the four winds, from the ends of the earth to the ends of heaven.

—Mark 13:24–27

Now what death is to each man, the Second Coming is to the whole human race.

—C. S. Lewis, from *The World's Last Night*

I do not know how many future generations we can count on before the Lord returns.

—James Watt, quoted in the *Boston Globe*, May 2, 1982

In a Time/CNN poll of 1,000 adult Americans conducted on April 28–29, 1993, by Yankelovich Partners Inc., 20% answered yes to the question, "Will the second coming of Jesus Christ occur sometime around the year 2000?" In addition, 49% answered no and 31% were not sure.

—Bernard McGunn, from *AntiChrist, Two Thousand Years of the Human Fascination with Evil*

The doctrine of the Second Coming is deeply uncongenial to the whole evolutionary or developmental character of modern thought. We have been taught to think of the world as something that grows slowly toward perfection, something that "progresses" or "evolves." Christian Apocalyptic offers us no such hope. It does not even foretell . . . a gradual decay. It foretells a sudden, violent end imposed from without; an extinguisher popped onto the candle, a brick flung at the gramophone, a curtain rung down on the play—"Halt!"

—C. S. Lewis, from *The World's Last Night*

. . . . .

SECULAR ESCHATOLOGY

From art and advertising to fitness, sports, and personal growth, many nonreligious aspects of our culture are marked by the images, language, as well as the expectations of apocalypticism and the end of days. Leached of the blood and judgment of its religious origins, secular eschatology can nevertheless still glow with a sense of crisis, judgment, ending, and foreboding.

This was Armageddon for the Knicks, an apocalyptic moment for the Pacers.

—Walt Frazier, on WFAN, New York, May 20, 1995

The question of whether the world will end in fire or in ice, with a bang or a whimper, no longer interests artists alone. Impending disaster has become an everyday concern, so commonplace and familiar that nobody any longer gives much thought to how disaster might be averted.

—Christopher Lasch, from *The Culture of Narcissism*

"I predict the world will come to an end in 1999 A.D."—Nostradamus, 16th Century astrologer. This leaves you five years to achieve your dream career. The School of Visual Arts offers 11 programs . . . your life is in your hands.

—from advertisement on New York City subway, 1994

. . . . .

SELF

I am the Self, seated in the hearts of all creatures, I am the beginning, the middle, and the end of all beings.

—*Bhagavad Gita*, 10:20

Après nous le déluge. [After us the flood.]

—Madame de Pompadour

There is no human problem which could not be solved if people would simply do as I advise.

—Gore Vidal

The end of humanity will come when everyone is like me, I declared one day in a fit I have no right to identify.

—E. M. Cioran, from *Anathemas and Admirations*

. . . . .

SERIOUSNESS

The end of all things is near; therefore be serious.

—1 Peter 4:7

Not famine, not pestilence, not war will bring back seriousness. . . . It is not till the eternal punishments of hell regain their reality that man will turn serious.

—Søren Kierkegaard

. . . . .

SEVEN

The magical number—seven seals, seven visions—also the organizing number, which, in the opinion of many interpreters, is the key to the structure of the Bible's last and most enigmatic book— Revelation.

The Apocalypse of St. John is the majestic image of a high and stately tragedy, shutting up and intermingling her solemn scenes and acts with a sevenfold chorus of hallelujahs and harping symphonies.

—John Milton, from *The Reason of Church Government*

I think the world is going to blow up in seven years. The public is entitled to a good time during those seven years.

—Henry Luce, in 1960, quoted in the *Washington Post Magazine*, Dec. 26, 1982

Then the world shall be turned back to primeval silence for seven days, as it was at the first beginnings, so that no one shall be left. After seven days the world that is not yet awake shall be roused, and that which is corruptible shall perish.

—2 Esdras 7:30–31

. . . . .

The Seventies (1970s)

Nixon's America and Ronald Reagan's California were doing their best to fall apart around us. Disaster was so omnipresent in our everyday view of things that we didn't even question its imminent arrival. We only wondered when and in what form it would come. Would it come as nuclear war? As a shift of the axis predicted by Edgar Cayce? As a great giggle of earth quaking like a fat Buddha at the size of the joke? Even if we had been sober we could not have conceived of the continuation of the world mess into the 1980s. We breathed eschatology the way we smoked cigarettes.

—Andrei Codrescu, from *In America's Shoes*

. . . . .

SEX

If you wanted to get America destroyed, if you were a malevolent, evil force, and you said, "How can I turn God against America? What can I do to get God mad at the people of America to cause this great land to vomit out the people?" Well, I'd pick five things. I'd begin to have incest, I'd begin to commit adultery wherever possible. I'd begin to have them offering them up and killing their babies. I'd get them having homosexual relations and I'd have them having sex with animals.

—Pat Robertson, quoted in the *San Francisco Examiner*, Sept. 7, 1986

The female sex is not a defect, but a natural state, which will then [at the time of resurrection] know no intercourse or childbirth. There will be female parts, not suited to their old use, but to a new beauty, and this will not arouse the lust of the beholder, for there will be no lust, but it will inspire praise of the wisdom and goodness of God.

—St. Augustine, from *City of God*

BIEBERMAN: . . . No one has properly realized the effect of all that exposed and quivering flesh on the national character. And my generation is condemned to watch this country, representing one of the greatest social experiments in Western civilization, choke itself to death on an easy diet of tits and asses?

—Bruce Jay Friedman, from *Steambath*

. . . . .

SIBYLLINE ORACLES

Next to Revelation and the book of Daniel, these collections of prophecies, allegedly uttered by Roman future-casting sibyls as inducements to conversion, were a third highly influential and very popular source of apocalyptic literature and visions in the ancient world. An amalgam of pagan, Jewish, and eventually, predominantly Christian materials, they were regularly revived throughout the Middle Ages.

A single day will see the burial of mankind, all that the long forbearance of fortune has produced, all that has been raised to eminence, all that is famous and all that is beautiful; great thrones, great nations—all will descend into one abyss, all will be overthrown in one hour.

—from the *Sibylline Oracles*

. . . . .

SIGNS AND PORTENTS

And you will hear of wars and rumors of wars; see that you are not alarmed; for this must take place, but the end is not yet. For nation will rise against nation, and kingdom against kingdom, and there will be famines and earthquakes . . . all this is but the beginning of the birthpangs.

—Matthew 24:6–8

> The blood-dimmed tide is loosed, and everywhere
> The ceremony of innocence is drowned;
> The best lack all conviction, while the worst
> Are full of passionate intensity.

—William Butler Yeats, from "The Second Coming"

Talk of portents was rife. Blood rained from the sky at noon, at night the deserted streets shook with the thunder of unearthly hoofbeats and weird cries filled the air. A woman at Ostia come to her time brought forth an issue of rats. Some said it was the reign of Antichrist, and that the end was nigh.

—John Banville, from *Doctor Copernicus*

A panic terror of the end of the world seized the good people of Leeds [England] and its neighborhood in the year 1806. It arose from the following circumstances. A hen, in a village close by, laid eggs, on which were inscribed the words, *"Christ is coming."* Great numbers visited the spot, and examined these wondrous eggs, convinced that the day of judgment was near at hand. . . . But a plain tale soon put them down. . . . Some gentlemen, hearing of the matter, went one fine morning and caught the poor hen in the act of laying one of her miraculous eggs. They soon ascertained beyond doubt that the egg had been inscribed with some corrosive ink, and cruelly forced up again into the bird's body.

—Charles Mackay, from *Extraordinary Popular Delusions and the Madness of Crowds*

. . . . .

SILENCE

When the Lamb opened the seventh seal, there was silence in heaven for about half an hour.

—Revelation 8:1

We suffocate among people who think they are absolutely right, whether in their machines or their ideas. And for all those who can live only in an atmosphere of human dialogue . . . this silence is the end of the world.

—Albert Camus, from "Neither Victims nor Executioners"

We are afraid
Of pain but more afraid of silence; for no nightmare
Of hostile objects could be as terrible as this void.
This is the abomination. This is the wrath of God.

—W. H. Auden, from "For the Time Being: A Christmas Oratorio"

. . . . .

SIMULTANEITY

Many times the cinema has tried to imagine a nuclear attack upon a city. What the cinema cannot get, what *we* cannot get, is the simultaneity: everything becoming nothing all at once.

—Martin Amis, from *Visiting Mrs. Nabokov and Other Excursions*

. . . . .

Six Six Six

This calls for wisdom: let anyone with understanding calculate the number of the beast, for it is the number of a person. Its
number is six hundred sixty-six.

—Revelation 13:18

"Three sixes."

"Six is a sign of the devil."

"Why three of them?"

"The diabolical trinity: the devil, anti-christ, and false
prophet. For everything holy there is something unholy. This is
the essence of temptation."

—from *The Omen*, film written by David Seltzer,
directed by Richard Donner

"What can the mark of the beast mean? It's the bar code, the
ubiquitous bar code on every box and pot pie. Every fuckin' bar
code is divided into three parts by two markers and those markers are always represented by the number six. Six six six. No one
shall buy or sell without that mark!"

—from *Naked*, film written and directed by
Mike Leigh

. . . . .

THE SIXTIES (1960s)

I believed my girlfriend was a witch. I believed my parents were Nazi space monsters. I believed the university was putting saltpeter in the cafeteria food. I believed stones had souls. I believed the NLF were the good guys in Vietnam. I believed Lyndon Johnson was plotting to murder all the Negroes. I believed Yoko Ono was an artist. I believed Bob Dylan was a musician. I believed I would live forever or until twenty-one, whichever came first. I believed the world was about to end.

—P. J. O'Rourke, from "Second Thoughts About the 1960s," in *Give War a Chance*

. . . . .

SKEPTICS

First of all you must understand this, that in the last days scoffers will come, scoffing and indulging their own lusts and saying, "Where is the promise of his coming? For ever since our ancestors died, all things continue as they were from the beginning of creation."

—2 Peter 3:3–4

More than any time in history mankind faces a crossroads. One path leads to despair and utter hopelessness, the other to total extinction. Let us pray that we have the wisdom to choose correctly.

—Woody Allen

. . . . .

SODOM AND GOMORRAH

Then the Lord rained on Sodom and Gomorrah sulphur and fire from the Lord out of heaven . . . and [Abraham] . . . saw the smoke of the land going up like the smoke of a furnace.

—Genesis 19:24–27

Modern day Sodoms are New York City, San Francisco, Amsterdam, Los Angeles . . . well, basically anywhere the population is over 50,000. The only reason that God has not destroyed these modern day Sodoms is that Catholic nuns and priests live in these cities, and God does not wish to destroy them. He does, however, give these people body lice and hepatitis.

—Christopher Durang, from
Sister Mary Ignatius Explains It All for You

Remember Sodom and Gomorrah!
It shall soon be the same again!

—from suicide note sent by Luc Jouret and the Order
of the Solar Temple, 1994

. . . . .

SOLAR SYSTEM

All the noon-day brightness of human genius is destined to extinction in the vast death of the solar system, and that the whole temple of man's achievement must inevitably be buried beneath the debris of a universe in ruins—all these things if not quite beyond dispute are yet so nearly certain that no philosophy which rejects them can hope to stand.

—Bertrand Russell, from *Mysticism and Logic*

. . . . .

SOLITUDE

For in all places there shall be great solitude; a person will long to see another human being, or even to hear a human voice.

—2 Esdras 16:26–27

The vast annihilation that has swallowed all things—the voiceless solitude of the once busy earth—the lonely state of singleness which hems me in. . . .

—Mary Shelley, from *The Last Man*

. . . . .

SPACE EXPLORATION

The sun, the moon, and the stars would have disappeared long ago had they happened to be within the reach of predatory human hands.

—Havelock Ellis

There is a space race down here on the ground. . . . Other species are bound to this or that patch of turf, and this planet. We feel bound to no patch or turf on Earth, bound only for the stars. We sacrifice a marsh, a bay, a park, a lake. We sacrifice a sparrow. We trade one countdown for another.

—Jonathan Weiner, from *The Next One Hundred Years*

For of course it is no very new idea that the eternal Son may, for all we know, have been incarnate in other worlds than earth and so saved other races than ours. . . .

But let us thank God that we are still very far from travel to other worlds.

. . . I have wondered before now whether the vast astronomical distances may not be God's quarantine precautions. They prevent the spiritual infection of a fallen species from spreading.

—C. S. Lewis, from *The World's Last Night*

. . . . .

SPECIES EXTINCTION

The disappearance of our species would be a distinct relief for the universe. Soon after extinction, its ominous history would be totally forgotten. There are insects better able to leave more permanent and less fatal traces of their passage than those left behind by the human race.

—Alvaro Mutis, from *The Adventures of Maqroll*

I don't think the human species will ever go extinct. I think we'll find the wisdom to put ourselves on the course of near-infinite tenancy of the earth.

—Edward O. Wilson, quoted in the *New York Times*, March 14, 1995

In sum, a full-scale nuclear attack on the United States would devastate the natural environment on a scale unknown since early geological times, when, in response to natural catastrophes whose nature has not been determined, sudden mass extinctions of species and whole ecosystems occurred all over the earth. . . . It appears that at the outset the United States would be a republic of insects and grass.

—Jonathan Schell, from *The Fate of the Earth*

Hitherto man had to live with the idea of death as an individual; from now onward mankind will have to live with the idea of its death as a species.

—Arthur Koestler

Myth: We have to save the earth. Frankly, the earth doesn't need to be saved. Nature doesn't give a hoot if human beings are here or not. The planet has survived cataclysmic and catastrophic changes for millions upon millions of years. Over that time, it is widely believed, 99 percent of all species have come and gone while the planet has remained.

Saving *the* environment is really about saving *our* environment—making it safe for ourselves, our children and the world as we know it. If more people saw the issue as one of saving themselves, we would probably see increased motivation and commitment to actually do so.

—Robert M. Lilienfeld and William L. Rathje from
"Six Enviro-Myths," in the *New York Times*, Jan. 21, 1995

. . . . .

SPECTACLE

For to see a World perishing in Flames, Rocks melting, the Earth trembling, and a Host of Angels in the Clouds, one must be very much a Stoick, to be a cold and unconcern'd Spectator of all this.

—Thomas Burnet, from *The Sacred Theory
of the Earth*

But what a spectacle is the impending advent of our Lord! . . . What will be that exultation of angels! What the glory of the rising saints, what thereafter the kingdom of the just! What the city New Jerusalem! But there will remain other spectacles; that day of judgment last and unending, that day unlooked for by the nations, that day derided, when the so great age of the world and all its productions will be consumed in one fire.

—Tertullian, from *On the Spectacles*

It [the End] would be not only the last, but also the finest show on earth, because it would be a perfect combination of aesthetic and moral spectacle. The elect would discuss it endlessly down the vistas of eternity and jubilantly extol this ideal mixture of destruction and retribution.

—Perry Miller, from *Errand into the Wilderness*

. . . . .

Spinning

"Do you feel there's any hope for the world?"

"No! As long as the world is turning and spinning, we'll be dizzy and nauseous and make mistakes. If some smart guy can stop it, then we'll be able to think and can solve all the problems. Good night!"

—Mel Brooks and Carl Reiner, from *The 2,013-Year-Old Man*

Stand still, you ever-moving spheres of heaven,
That time may cease, and midnight
never come.

—Christopher Marlowe, from *The Tragical History of Doctor Faustus*

. . . . .

Sports

Perhaps because the eschatological drama, as exemplified by the Christian story, is at heart a rough-and-tumble competition between close contenders—good and evil, Christ and Antichrist, eternal life and eternal damnation—the argot easily and uncannily lends itself to sports talk.

Four wins is a millennium. This is the toughest team we've faced.

> —Pat Riley, coach of the New York Knicks, quoted in
> the *New York Times*, June 7, 1994

Outlined against a blue-gray October sky, the Four Horsemen rode again. In dramatic lore they were known as Famine, Pestilence, Destruction, and Death. These are only aliases. Their real names are Stuhldreher, Miller, Crowley, and Layden.

> —Grantland Rice, from a story on Notre Dame
> football victory over Army (these players subsequently
> became known as the Four Horsemen of Notre Dame)
> in the *New York Tribune*, Oct. 18, 1924

The Final Four was the culminating event of the postseason collegiate basketball tournaments (then under way), and by its very name—it logically might have been dubbed the Top Four or even the First Four—the Final Four conveyed, not unlike AIDS and the Middle East, a sense of finality, entropy, apocalypse, something forcibly drawing to a close. . . . America had termination on the brain like a tumor.

> —Tom Robbins, from *Skinny Legs and All*

. . . . .

STAR WARS

This imaginative embrace of the heavens as a pristine alternative to chaos of life on earth, long since undermined by the Wright brothers, has collapsed totally in the era of Star Wars.

Space retains its symbolic power, but now as a vast stage set on which the deadly drama of cold war technological competition can be enacted.

—Paul Boyer, from "How S.D.I. Will Change Our
Culture," in *The Nation*, Jan. 10, 1987

And war broke out in heaven; Michael and his angels fought against the dragon. The dragon and his angels fought back, but they were defeated, and there was no longer any place for them in heaven. The great dragon was thrown down, that ancient serpent, who is called the Devil and Satan, the deceiver of the whole world—he was thrown down to the earth, and his angels were thrown down with him.

—Revelation 12:7–9

. . . . .

STATISTICS

[President John F.] Kennedy said that if we had nuclear war, we'd kill 300 million people in the first hour. [Secretary of Defense] McNamara, who is a good businessman and likes to save, says it would be 200 million.

—Norman Thomas

The death of one man is a tragedy. The death of millions is a statistic.

—Joseph Stalin, in a comment to Churchill
at Potsdam

· · · · ·

STOICISM

Not to hope for things to last for ever, is what the year teaches and even the hour which snatches a nice day away.

—Horace, from *Odes*

The sun stops. It is a minute past noon. Immediately, everything built by man collapses on the living and buries them. Only that which has a semblance of mechanical life lasts two seconds more. We see trains roll to the end of their course, machines turning empty, planes falling like dead leaves.

—Blaise Cendrars, from *The End of the World*
According to the Angel N.D.

That's great, It starts with an earthquake
Birds and snakes and airplanes
And Lenny Bruce is not afraid
. . . It's the end of the world as we know it
(and I feel fine).

—R.E.M., from "It's the End of the World As We
Know It (And I Feel Fine)"

· · · · ·

SUICIDE

Civilizations die of suicide, not by murder.

—Arnold Toynbee, from *A Study of History*

In the whole animal kingdom I recollect no family but man, steadily and systematically employed in the destruction of itself.

—Thomas Jefferson, in a letter to Madison

And in those days people will seek death but will not find it; they will long to die, but death will flee from them.

—Revelation 9:6

Hurry, my children, hurry. They will start parachuting out of the air. They'll torture our children. Lay down your life with dignity. Let's get gone. Let's get gone.

—Jim Jones, to the members of People's Temple, Guyana, 1978

The chaos of this world inescapably leads humanity toward the failure of its destiny.

Our transition will only appear to be a suicide in human terms. . . . We leave this world with unfathomable love, unspeakable joy, no regret whatever. Man, don't weep for our fate, but cry instead for your own.

—suicide note from Luc Jouret and the Order of the Solar Temple, 1994

Martyrdom offers the opportunity of personal salvation, though the world be lost. . . . This is certainly the logic of Jonestown, and possibly operated at Masada as well . . . mass death was a performance of the end of the world.

—Ted Daniels, from *Millennial Prophecy Report*

. . . . .

SUN AND STARS

Immediately after the suffering of those days the sun will be darkened, and the moon will not give its light; the stars will fall from heaven, and the powers of heaven will be shaken.

—Matthew 24:29

By watching, I know that the stars are not going to last. I have seen some of the best ones melt and run down the sky. Since one can melt, they can all melt; since they can all melt, they can all melt the same night. That sorrow will come—I know it. I mean to sit up every night and look at them as long as I can keep awake; and I will impress those sparkling fields on my memory, so that by and by when they are taken away I can by my fancy restore those lovely myriads to the black sky and make them sparkle again, and double them by the blur of my tears.

—Mark Twain, from *The Diary of Adam and Eve*

The last supernova in our galaxy was watched by Kepler in 1604. . . . Let's hope the next cosmic bomb doesn't go off too close to us. It could be calamitous for life on Earth, because the atomic radiation pouring into space from a nearby supernova would create conditions resembling all-out nuclear war.

—Nigel Calder, from *Violent Universe*

. . . . .

SURVIVALISM

I observed a pouring out of virtuous people from the metropolitan centers into the hinterlands. I beheld covenant communities standing separate from a tyrannical government. . . . It was Armageddon. Millions of massed soldiers—both men and women—were slaughtered, but the homeland was spared.

—James (Bo) Gritz, quoted in *Newsweek*, Sept. 5, 1994

"Hiding up in the hills like this seems so un-American."
"We're not staying here forever. When the shit hits the fan, we're coming down and taking over. Now you can't get any more American than that."

—from *Survivors*, film written by Michael Leesan,
directed by Michael Ritchie

Life—life the continuation of our animal mechanism—was the Alpha and Omega of the desire, the prayers, the prostrate ambition of the human race.

—Mary Shelley, from *The Last Man*

As of 1981, according to an account in the *New York Times*, a real-estate office in La Verkin, Utah, was offering for $39,000 a one-bedroom twelve-by-thirty-foot "unit" with blastproof doors and eight-inch reinforced-concrete ceilings, as well as a four-year supply of food.

—Otto Friedrich, from *The End of the World:*
A History

ATHENIAN: Then what view do you both take of the ancient legends? Have they any truth behind them?

CLINIAS: Which legends might you mean?

ATHENIAN: Those which tell of repeated destructions of mankind by floods, pestilences, and from various other causes, which leave only a handful of survivors. . . . The few who then escaped the general destruction must all have been mountain shepherds, mere scanty embers of humanity.

—Plato, from *Laws*

T

TABLOIDS

She picked up another tabloid. The cover story concerned the country's leading psychics and their predictions for the coming year. She read the items slowly.

. . . Earth's only satellite, the moon, will explode on a humid night in July, playing havoc with tides and raining dirt and debris over much of our planet. But UFO clean-up crews will help avert a worldwide disaster, signalling an era of peace and harmony.

—Don DeLillo, from *White Noise*

. . . . .

TELEVISION

If Christ had been put on television to preach the Sermon on the Mount, viewers would either have switched onto another channel, or contented themselves with remarking that the speaker had an interesting face. Christ might have become a television personality, but there would have been no Christianity.

—Malcolm Muggeridge, quoted in *The Causes of World War Three*

When we got our first TV in the 1940s or 1950s, I knew instantly that next to the atomic bomb this was the most important invention of our time.

—Newton Minow, in an NPR interview, July 12, 1995

A voice said to me, Tell the people the truth.

I said, What the hell do I know about the truth? What is this for godsake, the Burning Bush? I'm not Moses.

And the voice said, What's that got to do with it! I'm not God! We're not talking about permanent or ultimate truth, we're talking about transient human truth. . . .

And I said, Why me?

And the voice said, Because you're on television, dummy. There are 40 million listening. After tonight there will be 50 million.

—from *Network*, film written by Paddy Chayevsky, directed by Sidney Lumet

Television is the death throes of human consciousness.

—Don DeLillo, *White Noise*

. . . . .

TESTING

Men and ideas, the will and the spirit, are now being tested, perhaps in all truth for the final time; and in this testing so far, you Christians are standing in default.

—C. Wright Mills, from *The Causes of World War Three*

The Rebbe is testing us. If he had wanted to, he could have brought the Messiah long ago. He's taught us that the redemption comes after the darkest night. Our job is to get through the night.

—a teacher at Kfar Chabad, a Lubavitcher Chasidim village in Israel, quoted in *Forward*, March 18, 1994

. . . . .

TIME

Eschatologies in the Judeo-Christian scheme of things are predicated on a profound sense of linear time—that is, a sense of history as a story beginning with Once Upon a Time and proceeding to The End.

He ended; and thus Adam last replied:
How soon hath thy prediction, seer blest,
Measured this transient world, the race of time,

Till time stand fixed! Beyond is all abyss,
Eternity, whose end no eye can reach.

—John Milton, from *Paradise Lost*

Time touches all things with a destroying hand.

—Charles Waddell Chestnutt, from *The House
Behind the Cedars*

Thoughts, the slaves of life, and life, Time's fool,
And time, that takes survey of all the world,
Must have a stop.

—William Shakespeare, *Henry IV, Part One*

Modern thought has transferred the spectral character of
Death to the notion of time itself. Time has become Death tri-
umphant over all.

—John Berger, from *Keeping a Rendezvous*

Time is everything, man is nothing: he is at the most time's
carcass.

—Karl Marx, from *The Poverty of Philosophy*

The longest day must have its close—the gloomiest night will
wear on to morning. An eternal, inexorable lapse of moments is
ever hurrying the day of evil to an eternal night, and the night of
the just to an eternal day.

—Harriet Beecher Stowe, from *Uncle Tom's Cabin*

Lo, I am Time, that causes worlds to perish, grown mature, and come forth here to swallow up the world.

—*Bhagavad Gita* 22, 32

. . . . .

TOTALITARIANISM

The atom bomb, as the problem of mankind's very existence, is equalled by only one other problem: the threat of totalitarian rule (not simply dictatorship, Marxism, or racial theory), with its terroristic structure that obliterates all liberty and human dignity. By one, we lose life; by the other, a life that is worth living.

—Karl Jaspers, from *The Future of Mankind*

If you want a picture of the future, imagine a boot stamping on a human face—forever.

—George Orwell, from *1984*

. . . . .

TRAUMA

I mean the trauma suffered by everyone in the middle of the 20th Century when it became clear that from now on to the end of human history, every person would spend his individual life under the threat not only of individual death, which is certain, but of something almost insupportable psychologically—collective incineration and extinction which could come at any time, virtually without warning.

—Susan Sontag, from "The Imagination of Disaster,"
in *Against Interpretation*

Although there's a person we know all about
Still bearing our name and loving himself as before,
That person has become a fiction; our true existence
Is decided by no one and has no importance to love.

—W. H. Auden, from "For the Time Being: A
Christmas Oratorio"

. . . . .

TRIBALISM

The virus of tribalism . . . risks becoming the AIDS of international politics—lying dormant for years, then flaring up to destroy countries.

—from *The Economist,* July 6, 1991

. . . . .

TRIBULATION

In Premillennialism the period, usually interpreted as seven years in duration, of intense suffering, cosmic and political anarchy, epidemic, and disintegration usually occurring right after the Rapture inaugurating the Millennium and the last events.

When he opened the sixth seal . . . there came a great earth-quake; the sun became black as sackcloth; the full moon became like blood; and the stars of the sky fell to the earth as the fig tree drops its winter fruit when shaken by a gale. The sky vanished like a scroll rolling itself up, and every mountain and island was removed from its place. Then . . . everyone, slave and free, hid in the caves and among the rocks of the mountains.

— Revelation 6:12–15

. . . . .

TWENTIETH CENTURY

Just as I was thinking that no century could possibly be dumber than the nineteenth, along comes the twentieth. I swear, the entire planet seemed to be staging some kind of stupidity contest. I could tell then how the human story would end.

— Martin Amis, from *Einstein's Monsters*

U

UNBURIED

Those slain by the Lord on that day shall extend from one end of the earth to the other. They shall not be lamented, or gathered or buried; they shall become dung on the surface of the ground.

—Jeremiah 25:33

. . . . .

UNITED NATIONS

This organization [the U.N.] is created to prevent you from going to hell. It isn't created to take you to heaven.

—Henry Cabot Lodge, Jr., in the *New York Times,*
Jan. 18, 1954

The name of Christ is not mentioned at the close of prayer in the United Nations. In fact, Jesus has been excluded from the premises. Man has shut out the only hope of peace, according to the Bible. The spirit of "antichrist" reigns in the governments of the world.

—Hal Lindsey, from *The Late Great Planet Earth*

My fellow members of the United Nations Atomic Energy Commission, and my fellow Citizens of the World:

We are here to make a choice between the quick and the dead.

That is our business.

Behind the black portent of the new atomic age lies a hope which, seized upon with faith, can work our salvation. If we fail, then we have damned every man to be a slave of Fear. Let us not deceive ourselves: We must elect World Peace or World Destruction.

—Bernard M. Baruch, in a speech to the United Nations

. . . . .

UNRAVELING

He believed this: that the incomprehensible forces latent in matter innately possess a desire for release. That the universe is ever prepared to accomplish its own unmaking. That a thread dangles from the fabric of the world which if anyone were to grasp it would unravel the whole. *But this is what we all know.*

—Madison Smartt Bell, from *Waiting for the End of the World*

The world is unraveling out there like a cheap suit, and we've got to be ready.

> —from *Survivors*, film written by Michael Leesan,
> directed by Michael Ritchie

. . . . .

UNSIGNED

My theology, briefly, is that the universe was dictated but not signed.

> —Christopher Morley

. . . . .

UNZIPPING

Apocalypse happened in the year A.D. 2045. When I was sure it was coming I headed straight for the action: Tokyo. . . . I leased a top-floor room at the Century Inn near Tokyo Tower. . . . I bribed the floor guard and he gave me access to the roof: the final sleep-out. When I heard the sirens and the airwhine I sprang to my feet and stood there, nude, on tiptoe, with arms outstretched. And then it came, like the universe being unzipped.

> —Martin Amis, from *Einstein's Monsters*

. . . . .

UPWARD

If the world has not approached its end, it has reached a major watershed in history, equal in history to the turn from the Middle Ages to the Renaissance. It will demand from us a spiritual blaze. . . . No one on earth has any other way left but—upward.

—Aleksandr Solzhenitsyn, in *Solzhenitsyn at Harvard*,
Ronald Berman, ed.

. . . . .

UTOPIA

We have achieved utopia, *our* utopia, a utopia not of perfection but of comfort; and so the future disappeared. It simply vanished. It had to.

. . . Today, by dint of achieving the utopian future, we have lost our faith and see nothing.

—David Gelernter, from *1939: The Lost World
of the Fair*

We are at a curious juncture in the history of human insanity; in the name of realism, men are quite mad, and precisely what they call utopian is now the condition of human survival.

—C. Wright Mills, from *The Causes of
World War Three*

If people would forget about utopia! When rationalism destroyed heaven and decided to set it up here on earth, that most terrible of all goals entered human ambition. It was clear there'd be no end to what people would be made to suffer for it.

—Nadine Gordimer, in *Burgher's Daughter*

V

VIETNAM

It became necessary to destroy the town of Ben Tre to save it.

—Anonymous (attributed to a U.S. major in Vietnam),
in *The Observer*, Feb. 11, 1968

You don't believe we're on the eve of destruction.

—Barry McGuire, from "The Eve of Destruction"

. . . . .

VIOLENCE

The most terrible element in apocalyptic thinking is its certainty that there must be universal bloodshed.

—Frank Kermode, from *The Sense of an Ending*

The nature of the forces which the Lord will unleash on that day against the armies gathered in the Middle East is described in Zechariah 14:12: "And this shall be the plague wherewith the Lord will smite all the people that have fought against Jerusalem; Their flesh shall consume away while they stand upon their feet, and their eyes shall consume away in their holes, and their tongue shall consume away in their mouth" (KJV).

A frightening picture, isn't it? Has it occurred to you that this is exactly what happens to those who are in a thermonuclear blast? It appears that this will be the case at the return of Christ.

—Hal Lindsey, from *The Late Great Planet Earth*

It is no concern of ours how you run your own planet. But if you threaten to extend your violence, this earth of yours will be reduced to a burned out cinder. Your choice is simple. Join us and live in peace or pursue your present course and face obliteration. We shall be awaiting your answer. The decision rests with you.

—from *The Day the Earth Stood Still*, film written by Edward North, directed by Robert Wise

That even an apocalypse can be made to seem part of the ordinary horizon of expectation constitutes an unparalleled violence that is being done to our sense of reality, to our humanity.

—Susan Sontag, from *AIDS and Its Metaphors*

David Koresh is a thug who interprets the Bible through the barrel of a gun.

—Alcohol, Tobacco, and Firearms officer, interviewed
on *Turning Point*, Aug. 3, 1994

. . . . .

VIRTUAL REALITY

For as the bread, which is from earth, receiving the invocation of God, is no longer common bread, but the eucharist, consisting of two realities, earthly and heavenly; so, also our bodies, receiving the eucharist, are no longer corruptible, having the hope of resurrection to eternity.

—Iraneus, from *Against Heresy*

This permeation of the real world by the fictional is a symptom of the moral decay of our post-millennial culture. . . . There can be little doubt that a large majority of us opposes the free, unrestricted migration of imaginary beings into an already damaged reality.

—Salman Rushdie, from *East, West*

WAITING

But about that day or hour no one knows, neither the angels in heaven, nor the Son, but only the Father. Beware, keep alert; for you do not know when the time will come.

—Mark 13:32–33

> Ah! what time wilt thou come? when shall that crie
>   The Bridegroome's Coming! fil the sky?
>   Shall it in the Evening run
>   When our words and works are done?
> Or will thy all-surprizing light
>   Break at midnight?

—Henry Vaughn, from "The Dawning"

Now in these dread latter days of the old violent beloved U.S.A. and of the Christ-forgetting Christ-haunted death-dealing

Western world I came to myself in a grove of young pines and a question came to me: has it happened at last?

—Walker Percy, from *Love in the Ruins*

The expectation of apocalypse may be the occasion for a radical disaffiliation from society, as when thousands of Eastern European Jews in the 17th Century, hearing that Sabbatai Zevi had been proclaimed the Messiah and that the end of the world was imminent, gave up their homes and businesses and began the trek to Palestine.

—Susan Sontag, from "The Imagination of Disaster,"
in *Against Interpretation*

. . . . .

WALKS OF LIFE

Now the Lord is about to lay waste the earth and make it desolate, and he will twist its surface and scatter its inhabitants. And it shall be, as with the people, so with the priest; as with the slave, so with his master; as with the maid, so with her mistress; as with the buyer, so with the seller; as with the lender, so with the borrower; as with the creditor, so with the debtor.

—Isaiah 24:1–2

. . . . .

WAR

Proclaim this among the nations: Prepare war, stir up the warriors . . . Beat your plowshares into swords, and your pruning hooks into spears.

—Joel 3:9–10

We may inhabit the Indian summer of human history, with nothing to look forward to but the "nuclear winter" that closes the account. The war for which the great powers hold themselves in readiness every day may come, as hundreds of others have in the past. The megatons will fall, the dust will rise, the sun's light will fail, and the race may perish.

—Gwynne Dyer, from *War*

Mankind must put an end to war or war will put an end to mankind.

—John F. Kennedy

I do not know what weapons will be used in the next war, but the one after that will be fought with bows and arrows.

—Albert Einstein

Ever since the invention of gunpowder . . . I continually tremble lest men shall in the end uncover some secret which would provide a short way of abolishing mankind, of annihilating peoples and nations in their entirety.

—Baron Charles-Louis de Montesquieu, from *The Persian Letters*

. . . . .

WATERLESSNESS

It will come to pass with the upheaval of the earth that . . . deprived of the necessary supply of water . . . all the animals will perish, failing to find fresh grass for fodder . . . and it will come about after many desperate shifts that men will be forced to abandon their life and the human race will cease to be.

. . . Left arid and sterile, [the earth] having passed through the cold and rarefied air will be forced to end its course in the element of fire. Then the surface of it will remain burnt to a cinder, and this will be the end of all terrestrial nature.

—Leonardo da Vinci, from *The Notebooks of Leonardo da Vinci*, Edward MacCurdy, ed.

. . . . .

WEAR AND TEAR

O ruined piece of nature! This great world
Shall so wear out to nought.

—William Shakespeare, from *King Lear*

The ramparts of the great world also will be breached and collapse in crumbling ruin about us. Already, it is far past its prime. The earth, which generated every living species and once brought forth from its womb the bodies of huge beasts, has now scarcely strength to generate animalcules.

—Lucretius, from *On the Nature of Things*

The world looks worse every day. Is it worse, or does it just look it? It gets older. The world . . . has seen and done it all. Boy, is it beat. . . . The world has been to so many parties, been in so many fights, lost its keys, and had its handbag stolen, drunk too much. It all adds up. A tab is presented.

—Martin Amis, from *Einstein's Monsters*

. . . . .

WEATHER

There is no extended weather forecast today . . . which probably means there is no future.

—Steve Post, on WNYC, New York, Jan. 14, 1995

. . . . .

WHIMPERING

This is the way the world ends
Not with a bang but a whimper.

—T. S. Eliot, from "The Hollow Men"

. . . . .

WORD

In the beginning was the Word, and the Word was with God, and the Word was God. He was in the beginning with God. All things came into being through him, and without him not one thing came into being.

—John 1:1–3

What are you doing? [to a man in a London alley putting up posters cancelling shows] Cancelling everything? In the beginning was the word and the word was Cancelled!

—from *Naked*, film written and directed by
Mike Leigh

The world is but a word;
Were it all yours to give it in a breath,
How quickly were it gone!

—William Shakespeare, from *Timon of Athens*

. . . . .

WORLD GOVERNMENT

The late Arnold Toynbee of Cambridge foresaw that "only a world government can save mankind from annihilation by nuclear weapons." That's right! And Jesus Christ will be the King over all the earth in His theocratic world government.

—Billy Graham, from *Approaching Hoofbeats*

What is plain to me is that the modern world-state which was a mere dream in 1900 is today a practicable objective; it is indeed the only sane political objective for a reasonable man; . . . the way is indicated and the urgency to take that way gathers force. Life is now only conflict or "meanwhiling" until it is attained.

—H. G. Wells, from "The Idea of a Planned World,"
in *Experiment in Autobiography*

. . . . .

WORLD'S FAIR

[The 1939 World's Fair] was the Daniel, Ezekiel, Isaiah, Revelation of the American religion. Not the basic meat-and-potatoes but the ecstatic closing vision. The fair laid out the end of days. And having studied the fair, I think we will see that we are adrift, at least in part, because we are no longer marching toward utopia: We no longer can, because we are *in* it.

—David Gelernter, from *1939:*
The Lost World of the Fair

. . . . .

WORLD WAR TWO

Perhaps 51 million human beings were killed in the worldwide war that raged from 1939 to 1945. Bombed, fire-bombed, strafed, mined, suffocated, gassed, incinerated, frozen, mutilated, starved, beheaded, hanged, buried alive and dissolved in a luminous flash. Certainly more than half of them died as civilians.

—E. L. Doctorow, from "Mythologizing the Bomb," in
The Nation, Aug. 14, 1995

Military alliances, balances of power, leagues of nations, all in turn failed, leaving the only path to be by way of the crucible of war. The utter destructiveness of war now blocks out this alternative. We have had our last chance. If we will not devise some greater and more equitable system, Armageddon will be at our door.

—Douglas MacArthur, on accepting the Japanese
surrender, Sept. 2, 1945

. . . . .

WORLD WAR THREE

The Third World War was widely expected to be the first nuclear war—and perhaps the last. It turned out in the event to be essentially a war of electronics. . . . We can only be thankful to have survived, and wait and see.

—Sir John Hackett and others, from
The Third World War: August 1985

. . . . .

WRITING

Poetry has injured Religion in many ways. . . . Chiefly, it has wronged Religion by intruding its creative energy where it has no right of entry. There is no prophetical Hell. . . . The authors of apocalypses were poets, not prophets.

—Israel Abrahams, from *Poetry and Religion*

How can I continue to remain chained, day after day and far into the night, to this chair in a little room [in order to write] at a time when civilization threatens to destroy itself?

—Bernard Malamud, from "The Writer in the Modern World," unpublished lecture

Y

YEAR 1000

When I was a young man I heard a sermon about the End of the world preached before the people in the cathedral of Paris. According to this, as soon as the number of a thousand years was completed, the Antichrist would come and the last Judgment would follow in a brief time. I opposed this sermon with what force I could from passages in the Gospels, Revelation, and the Book of Daniel. . . . The rumor had filled almost the whole world that when the feast of the Annunciation coincided with Good Friday without doubt the End of the world would occur.

—Abbo of Fleury, from *Apologeticus*

. . . . .

YEAR 1666

After the Restoration, prophetic eyes were cast upon the calendrical collision of the number of the Beast of the Apocalypse, 666, with the millennial number, 1000. In that fantastic year

1000 plus 666, London was not transformed into the New Jerusalem but razed by a great fire while shiploads of Jews from Amsterdam headed toward Smyrna to join the Messiah, who had arrived at last in the figure of Sabbatai Zevi.

—Hillel Schwartz, from *Century's End*

. . . . .

YEAR 2000

Christianity, it will be recalled, is an eschatological faith whose story ends (literally) in apocalypse. Yet short of a miraculous second coming of the messiah, Christianity in the coming century will muddle on.

—James Davison Turner, from "That New-Time Religion," in *Tikkun* magazine March/April 1994

If we succeed, think how wonderful the year 2000 will be. And it is already so exciting to me that I am just hoping that my heart and stroke and cancer committees can come up with some good results that will insure that all of us can live beyond a hundred so we can participate in that glorious day when all the fruits of our labors and our imaginations are a reality.

—President Lyndon Baines Johnson, quoted in *Quotations from Chairman LBJ*, Jack Shephard and Christopher S. Wren, eds.

. . . . .

YEAR 3000

We can do it, you know.

We can get there. We can have it all. The Third Millennium A.D. can be the green millennium, the time in which we learn to live as responsible human beings at last.

There is no law, natural or divine, which demands that the world we live in become poorer, harsher and more dangerous. If it continues to become that way, it is only because we do it ourselves. . . .

—Isaac Asimov and Frederik Pohl, from
Our Angry Earth

Z

Zen

Form is no different from emptiness. Emptiness is no different from form. Form is precisely emptiness, emptiness is precisely form.

—from the Heart Sutra, in *The Little Zen Companion*,
David Schiller, ed.

Annihilating all that's made
To a green thought in a green shade.

—Andrew Marvell, from "The Garden"

THE BEGINNING

CREDITS

Allan Appel has published five novels, a biography, two collections of poetry, and several of his plays have been produced off Broadway. He lives in New York City, where he is also a false prophet, jogger, husband, and father. He does not want the world to end any sooner than it has to—certainly not before you read this book.